MUTUAL
by
DESIGN

A Better Model for Christian Marriage

General Editor
Elizabeth Beyer

Contributing Editor
Lynne Nelson

CBE International
www.cbeinternational.org

Mutual by Design: A Better Model for Christian Marriage

Published by CBE International
122 W Franklin Ave, Suite 218
Minneapolis, MN 55404
www.cbeinternational.org

All Scripture quotations, unless otherwise noted, are taken from THE HOLY BIBLE, NEW INTERNATIONAL VERSION®, NIV® Copyright © 1973, 1978, 1984, 2011 by Biblica, Inc.™ Used by permission. All rights reserved worldwide.

ISBN: 978-1-939971-70-8 (Print)
ISBN: 978-1-939971-71-5 (PDF)
ISBN: 978-1-939971-72-2 (Mobi)
ISBN: 978-1-939971-73-9 (ePub)

Cover design by Jessica Hillstrom Ess, HillSpring Books

Printed in the United States of America

Contents

Preface

At the beginning of creation, God made them male and female. Because of this, a man should leave his father and mother and be joined together with his wife, and the two will be one flesh." So they are no longer two but one flesh. (Mark 10:6–8, CEB)

Marriage. It's been around for millennia, so what more can be said that hasn't already been said? Many books on Christian marriage have been written, but most assume that the Bible puts men in a leadership role, while women are to be submissive. But there's a better way. Not only is it healthier for families, but it's more faithful to the Bible. The Bible casts a vision of marriage where men and women co-lead and co-serve as equal partners. This book explores that vision.

Mutual by Design is divided into three sections. The first section, "In the Beginning," provides a biblical foundation for mutuality in marriage. The second section, "Nuts & Bolts," addresses the building blocks for growing a strong marriage, touching on topics such as how to develop friendship and intimacy; the key elements of good communication; the difference between forgiveness and reconciliation; and building a stable foundation financially. The final section, "What About...," examines three areas that have been difficult topics in the church—headship, abuse, and divorce. The content of these three chapters are included in this book in the hope that they will bring clarity to issues that have been confusing in the church.

This book is for those considering marriage, those already engaged, newlyweds, and any couple seeking to improve their relationship. The book can be used for individual couples or groups. Chapters include discussion questions, exercises, and suggestions for further reading.

Our gratitude goes out to those who have faithfully supported CBE International in developing this book through financial support, consultation, and prayer. Special thanks to Lynne Nelson, who generously offered her expertise and time in the early stages of the project.

Elizabeth Beyer
Minneapolis, October 2017

GENESIS

A Very Good Place to Start

– 1 –

Back to the Beginning
Man and Woman in the Image of God

Manfred T. Brauch

In the classic musical, *The Sound of Music*, the main character, Maria, is a governess caring for seven children. Her top priority is teaching the children to sing, so she invents a song to help them. Whether or not you've seen the musical, you've probably heard the song, called "Do-Re-Mi."

The song's opening line goes, "Let's start at the very beginning. A very good place to start." The rest of the song goes on to do just that, teaching the fundamentals of singing notes. Maria's strategy is a good one: start with the basics. She knows that if the children can master the basics, they could unlock their musical potential.

The same is true of marriage. When two people understand and embrace the fundamentals of marriage, they can discover a relationship of great potential. Unfortunately, Christians too often misunderstand God's design for marriage. As a result, we see abuse and widespread divorce, dissatisfaction, and discord.[1] We can do better. We can discover the pattern God created for marriage.

Like children learning to sing, in order to learn God's design for marriage, we need to start at the very beginning: creation.

The creation story found in the first chapters of Genesis is probably familiar to you. In six days, God fashions creation from nothing. Light from darkness. Water and land, day and night. Sun, moon, and stars. Plants, fish, and birds. On the sixth day, after filling the land with animals, God crafts his most precious creation: humanity.

> "So God created humankind in his image,
>   in the image of God he created them;
>   male and female he created them." (Gen. 1:27 NRSV)

At the climax of creation, humanity (and also male-female relationships), enter the scene. As the Biblical faith about God's creative work unfolds in the first three chapters of Genesis, we see God's design for human relationships and for marriage, and we witness sin tragically pervert that design.

In the early chapters of Genesis, some people find the beginnings of patriarchy—that is, a way of life where men hold power and authority over women. You've surely heard the basic points of this reading of the story: God made Adam in his image, to represent God on earth, to rule the earth, and do God's will. But what about Eve? After all, she was created second. Adam was the original human, and then God added Eve as a "helper" for Adam, confirming that God means for the man to lead while the woman follows, assists, and submits. This seems to be reinforced again when the first couple sins and God says to the woman, "he [the man] shall rule over you." It makes a lot of sense, doesn't it?

The problem with this version of humanity and marriage is that it's based on misinterpretaion of the biblical text. The first three chapters of Genesis actually reveal a different story, where the man and woman are equal partners in every way. Both male and female bear God's image and they share responsibility to rule the earth and do God's will. Together. Eve was not an afterthought because Adam needed an assistant. Like God rescues his people from calamity, God's creation of her rescued Adam from being alone—a devastating place to be for a human made in the image of a relational God. And God's statement that men would rule over women was a tragic outcome of sin, and not God's desire. This is the true story of Genesis, the foundation of Christian marriage.

Let us take a deeper look at each of these points.

Male, Female, and the Image of God

A colleague recently spoke at a conference in Tanzania about gender and the Bible. During the conference, several pastors in the back of the room remarked that women cannot be men's equals. "Man was created in God's image," they explained, "but woman was made from man. So women bear man's image, not God's." While this view is less common today in Western churches than in the rest of the world, it reflects church tradition. Many early church fathers and medieval theologians taught that, one way or another, women were made less in the image of God than men. Why does this matter, and what does Genesis actually tell us?

For centuries, people have debated what it means to be made in God's image. Some say it has to do with spiritual self-awareness and rational thought. Others say it means we are designed to be in relationship with other humans. Still others say it means God has placed us here to rule over the earth on his behalf. Whatever the exact meaning, it is clear that we are unique in creation, and in a variety of ways, we embody the character of God as we take care of creation. Being made in God's image gives us the utmost dignity and worth. Whatever we do to someone made in God's image, we also do to God.

Depending on which translation you read, Genesis tells us that either "man" or "mankind / humankind" was made in God's image. Which is correct? Do women bear only a secondary kind of image? To answer the question, we need to look at the Hebrew word so often translated as "man."

In English, Adam is a first name. Most people don't realize that it is simply an ancient Hebrew word, *adam*, which can mean "man" or "human being," just like the English word "man." It is also used in Genesis as the name of the first male human. But everywhere that Genesis talks about God's image, *adam* clearly refers not only to the man we call Adam, but to humanity:

Genesis 1:26 says "Let us make *adam* in our image... and let *them* have dominion..." Often, *adam* is translated as "man," but the plural pronoun "them" shows that here the word *adam* is used not as a designation of the individual male, but rather as a *generic noun*, referring to all *humanity*. This is why the NRSV translates it, "Let us make humankind in our image."[2]

Genesis 1:27 confirms this meaning of the Hebrew *adam* in the context of God's image:

> So God created *adam* in his image,
> in the image of God he created him,
> male and female he created *them*.

The structure of this passage is an example of "poetic parallelism" in the Hebrew language. The second line repeats the essential content of the first line, and the third line expands and clarifies the first two lines. The pronoun "him" in the second line refers back to the masculine singular noun, *adam*, in the first line. But as in 1:26, the plural pronoun "them" in the third line indicates that *adam* is used again as a generic noun, designating *humanity*.

Genesis 5:1-2 says that *adam* is created "in the likeness of God." It is clear that *adam* here, as in 1:26–27, is used as a generic noun, because it goes on to say, "Male and female he created them and blessed them and named them *adam* when they were created" (Gen. 5:2). Male and female together are designated as *adam*; both equally human and in the likeness of God.

It is significant that the "image of God" is bestowed on human beings jointly in their male-female forms and partnership. That is to say, it is ultimately only in the context of human relationships that the "image of God," the reflection of God's character and purpose, is realized. We are created in and for relationship.[3]

The male-female relationship is framed by an identity and task, unique to humans but shared by both male and female. Their unique identity results from their creation "in the image and likeness of God." They are designed as God's representatives, to "image," or reflect and embody, the character and purposes of God throughout the entire creation.[4] Their unique task is to "have dominion" over the rest of the created order. Both man and woman bear God's image. In this co-humanity, they are called to jointly exercise dominion and stewardship over, and within, creation.[5] There is no hint of second-class citizenship for one gender, and no indication of "functional inequality" where the man rules and leads and the woman submits and follows.

CREATION ORDER

You might have heard people say that one way we know Adam (the male) is meant to be the leader is because Adam was created first (according to Genesis 2). Eve was created second, to be a "helper" to Adam. In the next section, we'll talk about what it means that Eve was a "helper" to Adam. However, before we do, let's talk briefly about the relationship between Genesis 1 and Genesis 2 and the order of creation.

Some interpreters believe that Genesis 2 tells us about the specific sequence in the creation of male and female, which needs to be "inserted" into the Genesis 1:26–27 narrative to "explain" it. However, it is much more likely that whereas Genesis 1:26–27 expresses God's design for humanity as a whole in its male-female nature, Genesis 2 expresses the divine intention for the relationship between a man and a woman in the covenant of marriage.

So, in Genesis 2. what does it mean that Adam was created first? Does it mean that he should have leadership or authority over Eve? This idea of "chronological priority" is often called "the principle (or even *doctrine*) of primogeniture." Primogeniture is a term that describes the common practice in ancient Israel of giving the greatest blessing and inheritance to the first-born son. A preference for that which comes first was common in ancient Jewish culture (see the appendix for examples of this idea in writings by famous Jewish philosophers and early church fathers).

However, this isn't a good enough reason to assume that God meant men to be in charge. First, the Genesis account shows us a pattern where the last of a series is the most important. A church father named Gregory of Nyssa wrote about this, saying "Creation moves from lower to higher, to the perfect form, humanity."[6] We certainly see this in Genesis, where the creation of human beings, male and female, in God's own image is the climax of the whole creation.

This is confirmed by the fact that God gives humans authority over all of the rest of creation. Humans were the last thing God made, not the first. God's intent was clearly not to give authority to the earliest creations! This is not to say that the woman is more important than the man, but that *humanity* is the high point of creation.

Second, even the words of the story suggest a balance between male and female. In Hebrew, nouns have a grammatical gender, much like Spanish, French, German, and many other languages. In Genesis, the man (*adam*, masculine) emerges from the ground (*adamah*, feminine, Gen. 2:7). And the woman (*ishah*, feminine) emerges from the man (*ish*, masculine. Gen. 2:23). We have a similar balancing in 1 Corinthians 11:11–12, where Paul states that "just as woman came from man, so man comes through woman."

Finally, we need to remember that while a preference for the "first" may have been the norm in the culture of ancient Israel, it is something God often rejects! Repeatedly, God sets aside the cultural preference for "first" to accomplish his purpose: Isaac is chosen over Ishmael, Jacob over Esau, David over Saul. Jesus' word that "the last will be first and the first will be last" (Matt. 19:30; 20:16) articulates this biblical rejection of cultural preference.

WOMAN AS MAN'S "HELPER"

In the television drama series, *Downton Abbey*, we see a compelling story of early twentieth-century life on an English estate. The show revolves around an aristocratic family, the Crawleys, and their multitude of servants as they adapt to a changing society. The Crawleys' lifestyle depends entirely on their servants, who dress them, care for their children, cook their food, conceal their secrets, and everything in between. The servants need the Crawleys, too, because their work is their livelihood. The Crawleys and their servants don't only depend on each other, but often share mutual respect and affection. Yet, the line between family and servant is always clear, and that social order is not to be tampered with.

Compare this to a scene from the 2002 movie, *The Two Towers*, the second in the *Lord of the Rings* movie trilogy based on the classic Tolkien book of the same name. One of the key points in the film is a battle at the fortress called Helm's Deep. A small band of humans and elves faces off against an overwhelming army of evil forces. Just as it becomes clear that all hope is lost, the few remaining heroes look up at the nearby hilltops. As the sun rises, Gandalf the wizard appears over the ridge with an army of horsemen, and hope is restored. They turn the tide of the battle and good triumphs over evil once again.

What do these very different examples have in common? They both illustrate the idea of help. Which one comes closer to what you think of when you hear that God made Eve because no other suitable "helper" could be found for Adam (Gen. 2:18–23)?

In English, it's typical for "helper" to bring to mind something like "assistant" or "domestic helper" or "servant." It's easy to assume that Adam was in charge, and Eve was there to help out as needed.[7] But is that the true understanding of the story? Far from it! To understand why, we need to dig into the Hebrew words once again.

The meaning of the Hebrew word, translated "helper," simply cannot be squeezed into the meaning of "helper" as "assistant" or "servant."[8] The Hebrew phrase used in Genesis and translated as "suitable helper" is *ezer kenegdo*. Let's dig into this phrase, looking first at the word *ezer*.

Ezer is derived from the word **azar** (to help). *Azar* doesn't mean simply "to help," though. It indicates the action of someone who saves another from extreme danger, or who delivers another from death. The noun *ezer* is used to describe one person in relation to another twenty-one times in the Old Testament. Two of those are the ones in Genesis 2. Three more describe military protectors and rescuers.[9] Other than these five, *ezer* is only and always used for God as the redeemer who rescues from distress, danger, calamity, and death.[10]

Given what we know about the word *ezer*, it evokes something quite the opposite of a subservient role. The woman is depicted as the one created by God to liberate man from aloneness. Adam's aloneness was not a problem because he had no one to help him get his work done, but because being alone harms our very humanity. Recall that we humans, being made in the image of God, are relational to our core. Our God is a Trinity (Father, Son, and Spirit) who exists in what theologians call a "community of love." Humans are created to exist in a community of love as well. That is why it was "not good that the man should be alone" (Gen. 2:18). In no way does the word *ezer* connote the idea of the woman as man's assistant or subordinate.

The second word in the phrase translated as "suitable helper" is *kenegdo*, which means "fit for him" or "suitable for him." This term underlines the note of prominence and strength already expressed in the word *ezer*. *Kenegdo's* root word, *neged* means literally "in front of, in sight of, opposite to" (equivalent to the English expression "face to face"). The related Hebrew noun *nagid* designates a leader, ruler, prince (such as a general, "in front of" his troops, leading them into battle). It is clear that *kenegdo* points to Eve being an equal partner to Adam.[11]

As a whole, the Hebrew phrase *ezer kenegdo* ("helper suitable for him") designates the woman as the one whose creation and being leads the man out of his aloneness. Unlike the animals, who are found not to be man's *ezer kenegdo*, (Gen. 2:19–20), the woman does correspond to him; she is his equal partner, "flesh of my flesh and bone of my bones" (Gen. 2:23). Fashioned from the same essence and substance, she complements and completes him.[12]

The church father Chrysostom (CE 344–407) expresses the status of the woman before the fall, as intended by God, in these words:

> In the beginning I created you equal in esteem to your
> husband, and my intention was that in everything you
> would share with him as an equal; and as I entrusted
> control of everything to your husband, so did I to you.[13]

Armed with a better understanding of the Hebrew phrase *ezer
kenegdo*, we see a clearer picture of the relationship between
Adam and Eve. Theirs was nothing like a master-servant
relationship. Instead, we should picture Eve as a heroic rescuer
created by God, like Gandalf's army appearing over the hilltop.
She enables humanity to flourish as intended—in mutual
relationship with equal counterparts.

The Fall

The first two chapters of Genesis paint a picture of equality,
mutuality, and partnership in fulfilling God's mandate to
populate and steward the earth.[14] Tragically, Adam and Eve's
relationship becomes terribly distorted when they try to cross
God-given boundaries to become "like God" (Gen. 3:5). Their
quest for absolute knowledge and to transcend their limits has
the opposite result: humanity becomes less than fully human.
The consequences are disastrous for both man and woman.
Their relationship of equality and partnership becomes a
"power-over" relationship: "He will rule over you" (Gen. 3:16).

This account of the curse, including the man ruling over the
woman, has been understood by some as a divine command
for the nature of that relationship. However, this misses the
entire point of God's work in history.

The entire story of God's redemptive work—from the call of

Abraham (Gen. 12:1–3) and concluding with the vision of a new heaven and a new earth in which "nothing accursed will be found any more" (Rev. 22:3)—is the story of God working to *free* humanity and all of creation from its *cursed existence* (Rom. 8:19–23). In light of this, the curse of Genesis 3 has to be understood not as *prescriptive* (what *should* be) but as *descriptive*, revealing *what is* the human condition when separated from relationship with God and God's original intent.

It is also clear from the sweep of the biblical revelation that the people of God are called to participate in and embody this liberating, transforming work of God. Israel is called to be a "blessing" and a "light to the nations" (Gen. 12:2–3; Isa. 19:24–25, 42:6). The new covenant community of Jew and Gentile "in Christ" is to be God's alternative to the brokenness of fallen human society, including the distorted male-female relationship.

The curse is to be fought and overturned, not embraced. As followers of Christ, we are to restore the male-female mutuality, equality, and partnership that God designed. This is the marriage pattern we should pursue.

CONCLUSION

The texts we have examined—about the creation of humanity (*adam*) as male and female in God's image, the order of creation, the creation of the woman as man's "helper," and the cursedness of the man's rule over the woman—paint a clear picture of God's design for humanity, male and female, and for marriage.

We have seen that it is not only Adam who is created in God's image, but humanity itself, in both male and female forms. Not only do man and woman share a human essence, but they share in humanity's duty to populate and exercise responsible stewardship over creation. Throughout this creation narrative, we see it building to its climax in the creation of humans, in equal partnership with one another and in God's image, as the pinnacle of creation

And while in the Genesis 2 creation story Adam is created first, we've seen that this says nothing about leadership or rule or authority. So the Genesis 2 narrative confirms the affirmation of Genesis 1:26–27: God created male and female, together, in God's image.

We have also seen that Eve being Adam's helper does not indicate that she is his subordinate. Far from being an assistant, she is a strong rescue. She is God's instrument to save him from a tragic existence of alone-ness. She is his equal, his counterpart. Together, they can fully embody the image of our relational God.

This sets the stage for the fall in Genesis 3. The rule of the man over the woman (Gen. 3:16) is a dramatic departure from the order of creation. The Creator's good design and intent for the man-woman relationship has become twisted and distorted. The hierarchical over-under condition of the male-female relationship is "in bondage to sin." It was never God's design or desire.

Rescuing humanity from sin—sin that includes male rule over women—is the center of God's redeeming work, which culminates in Christ. Jesus' challenge to hierarchical power structures in human relationships, and Paul's conviction that "in Christ" we have been set free from enslavement to sin, are further evidence that male-female hierarchy is out of place in the new creation.[15]

Mutuality in marriage was God's design when the foundations of the earth were laid, and it remains God's desire to this day. Let us pursue God's way with all our strength.

QUESTIONS FOR REFLECTION AND DISCUSSION

1. Why is it important to start with the book of Genesis for a discussion on marriage?

2. How does properly understanding the concept of God's image change male/female relationships?

3. Is there any significance to the chronology of creation? Does it matter who comes first or last?

4. Although Genesis 1 and 2 differ from one another in some respects, what do they both affirm about humans?

5. Look up a few of the verses that reference the word ezer. How do these verses help the reader understand what a "helper" is?

6. What is the difference between prescriptive scripture and descriptive scripture, and how does this apply to the curse in Genesis 3?

7. What are the major ideas you will take away from this chapter?

"Nuts and Bolts" of Relationships

– 2 –

Intimate Friendship
How do we get there?

Janelle Kwee and Hillary McBride

"The voice is a window to the soul. The seat of the soul is not inside a person, or outside a person, but the very place where they overlap and meet the world"
—Gerard de Nerval

Noelle and Simon are in their early forties, have been married for fifteen years, and have three children between ages seven and twelve. Their middle child has special needs and requires numerous appointments, and all of the children are involved in sports and lessons outside of school. Noelle is often stressed out by deadlines in her job as a paralegal. Simon, a self-employed contractor, struggles to manage boundaries around his work, especially because he feels pressure to be the "breadwinner." Adding to their stress, Noelle's mother, who used to help with the children, is undergoing chemotherapy, and needs additional support. Finally, Simon serves on the board of their church which is undergoing a leadership transition; this commitment has made him more preoccupied and unavailable to his family. Date nights have been squeezed out of their schedule for some time. Simon and Noelle have started to feel like cohabitants in the same household and argue frequently about who should be doing what. While this couple is committed to each other, nurturing their marriage has come to feel like the last priority.

Does their story sound familiar to you? Perhaps Noelle or Simon is a friend of yours? Or maybe you can you see yourself in Noelle and Simon's story?

In this chapter, we will explore the topic of mutual, self-giving love in marriage through a discussion of friendship, intimacy, and spirituality. We start by reflecting on insights that the Trinity offers about our relationality as beings made in God's image, then discuss what closeness looks like in marriage, and explore practical considerations to deal with challenges. Finally, we offer questions for further reflection and discussion on your own, with your partner, or in small group discussion format. We hope to convey a sense of the importance and possibility of cultivating lifelong friendship and closeness as marriage partners.

Why Does Friendship and Intimacy Matter in Marriage?: Insights from the Trinity

Humans bear the image of God. This means that the nature of the triune God is the basis for understanding human relationship.[1] God is love, and we are also love and called to love. As we make loving connections with others, we discover our own humanity and truly reflect God's image. Each person of the Trinity is in perfect intimacy but also mysteriously maintains a separate self.[2] In the same way, acceptance and belonging in marriage are affirmed, where both separateness and "we-ness" coexist. Humans are created for relationship and designed to exist with intimacy in community.[3] The practical question is: what does healthy intimacy look like?

What does Healthy Friendship and Intimacy Look Like in Marriage? How can We get There?

When people refer to intimacy in marriage, often they are referring to sex and romantic expression. However, intimacy is so much more than our ability to be close to someone physically and sexually; it is also our ability to be close emotionally. Of course all these aspects of intimacy are part of a thriving marriage relationship, but here, we focus on the importance of drawing close to each other emotionally, to sustain a lifelong friendship and shared sense of purpose together.

The ability for a couple to thrive together in marriage cannot be reduced to a single process or skill. The core of a thriving and fulfilling marriage, and a couple's ability to endure the challenges of life, is a deep relational bond with several key characteristics: (1) safety and vulnerability; (2) a couple's enjoyment of each other; (3) each person's authenticity; and (4) shared meaning and purpose.[4]* A healthy marital bond involves two people who can create a safe place where each

---

*These characteristics parallel the elements of personal fulfillment described in Existential Analysis,[6] which can be summarized in the person's ability to say "yes" to four foundational questions in our existence: (1) Can I be? Do I experience the

one is fully seen and accepted as they are.

VULNERABILITY AND SAFETY

"Love is friendship set on fire"—Jeremy Taylor

Consider the metaphor of love as friendship ablaze: more than other friendships, love has a power that can give life or hurt life. To use that power to sustain and grow a marriage friendship, each partner has to be seen and safe. Being honest or authentic in a marriage doesn't permit a person to say whatever they want whenever they want. To really be together, each partner must have space, protection, and support. They must have both the emotional safety of being committed to each other, and safety from physical violence. Each partner has a responsibility to facilitate safety, protection, and support for the other, not based on gender roles that presume one to be stronger and one to be weaker. The vulnerability to be seen, known, and accepted is possible only when emotional safety is established. You can explore the theme of safety with these questions:

- Can I really be in this relationship or do I feel I tip-toe around the other person?
- Does my partner tip-toe around me?
- Is one of us more present than the other?
- Can I "take up space" to be myself in this relationship—in

---

necessary safe, protection, and support to be here?; (2) Do I like to live? Do I feel my emotions and feel goodness in my life?; (3) May I be my authentic self? Am I free to be me?; (4) For what am I here?; What gives my life meaning?

my own body, and with my own thoughts and feelings?

- Can I let my partner take up space to be him or herself, to have his or her own needs in our relationship?
- Do I feel a sense of rootedness, belonging, and acceptance?
- Do I offer a sense of acceptance, belonging, and rootedness to my partner?

It is difficult to cultivate a thriving and intimate relationship while keeping parts of ourselves hidden. When there is physical and emotional safety, each partner has the opportunity to explore the parts of themselves they are most tempted to hide, most afraid will be rejected, or which carry the most shame. Shame is the feeling that parts of us are unworthy, un-belonging, undeserving, and unlovable.[5] The paradox of shame is that in order for us to be healed, we must make known these parts that feel unlovable. Exposing our shame for the sake of healing can feel like being asked to step into traffic, but we can take the risk to expose our hearts and minds when we feel secure in a lifelong bond with our spouse.

Regardless of gender, skill, or supposed role in the marriage, we all participate in making a marriage meaningful. We do this by providing a safe place to be vulnerable for our spouse, and leaning into our own vulnerability. Most popular depictions of relationships, show vulnerability coming from the female. However, a person's emotional needs and expression have more to do with their temperament and experience than their gender. Despite what our culture teaches about how men and women are supposed to behave and feel, men need emotional safety as much as women do, and wives deserve to see and encounter their husband's emotional vulnerability. This requires us to step outside the script of popular culture and the church that women must be emotional (associated with weakness), and men must be stoic (associated with strength).

Unfortunately, boys learn from an early age in Western and patriarchal culture that their emotions, particularly sadness, need to be silenced, or cut off; thus, the process of building emotional intimacy may be uniquely challenging for some men.[6] This dichotomy that women are emotional and men are rational hurts both. Women's relative ease with sensing and sharing emotions has been used to silence, oppress, disempower, and discredit women. The argument that a woman can't think straight because of emotions dismisses the role of emotion in discernment and understanding. What about a man's capacity to be aware of his feelings when he has been deeply socialized to prioritize his rationality? A man deserves to embody his wholeness as a rational and emotional being in the same way that a woman deserves to embody wholeness as somebody who has both emotional and rational capacities.

A COUPLE'S ENJOYMENT OF EACH OTHER

Recall the vignette of Noelle and Simon. When they were dating, this couple used to stay up late at night, talking about the mundane things in life, sharing their painful, joyful, and hilarious memories—taking the time to really get to know each other. Like many couples, they did a beautiful job of building their friendship bond at the beginning of their relationship. The motivation to get up early to watch a sunrise, or to stay out late for a walk in the dark, came easily when things felt new and promising. However, this enjoyment of each other that is so common in the early stages of a relationship is not just because it is new, but also because of the deliberate energy each person puts into the other person.

When a relationship is new, we give this time to nurture it because we are aware that it holds promise of something good. While the warmth of building an exciting friendship seems to come naturally early in a relationship, it can become sidelined by other priorities. Like Simon and Noelle, couples often describe a shift from "fun" to "business" over the course of a committed relationship. To sustain friendship and intimacy, a couple must take time to enjoy and appreciate each other. You can explore the theme of enjoyment with the following questions:

- How do I feel with my partner?
- Do I feel my emotions in this relationship and experience goodness in our shared life?
- What is good in our life together?
- Do I feel a sense of connectedness with my spouse?
- What attracts me to this person or this relationship?
- When do I feel a sense of warmth and comfort with my partner?
- Does it feel good to be in this relationship?

Pondering these questions may seem threatening if the answers are negative. What if the spark is gone? What happens when you want to uphold your marriage vows but it seems that your relationship is defined by the mundane and by small resentments? Be reassured that it is not marital doom to "lose the spark." In fact, it is normal for people in a long-term committed relationship to feel a loss of warmth from time to time. Living in a perpetual state of relational coldness, however, is not sustainable. So, what can be done? First of all, being aware that you are missing the spark is an invitation to cultivate it again. Rather than focusing on the dwindling joy, notice your hunger for closeness and make time to give each other attention and appreciation—the things that came so naturally before.

Consider how often you check in with your partner to share or connect about small or big things. Consider how often you plan events to look forward to, or have rituals and favorite ways of spending time together. How often are these events a priority in your life? If you have children, how often do you get time away from the kids to nourish your marital bond? How often do you spend time alone together without discussing the kids at all? Commitment to one another is not enough to sustain connected friendship Restoring friendship and closeness sometimes requires help; reaching out for professional counseling may be a way to affirm the priority of (re)building your friendship.

EACH PERSON'S AUTHENTICITY

An opening exercise that we often carry out when seeing

couples for counseling is to draw a Venn diagram of two partially overlapping circles and label them "me" and "you," and write "'us" in the middle.

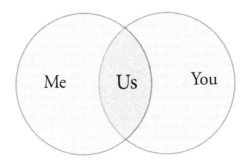

We do this to illustrate to couples that a marriage, the "us" part of the diagram, is something new made up of who you are, and who I am. While we can easily point to and identify the two people who make up the marriage, together those people create a new thing—a living relationship which demands nurture, care, and attention. Like a plant that needs watering, this living relationship requires certain things in order to be sustained. These include the elements we have been exploring such as safety, vulnerability, and time. Additionally, for the "we" part to be well, each individual person must be able to experience personal authenticity, to be able to be fully oneself.

Couples will often face difficulty when the overlap between their two individual selves is lacking. When the shared marital bond and identity is missing, couples describe feeling like they are living separate lives, like roommates, or like the only thing which reminds them they are married is their wedding band, and the bed they share. It is not unusual for couples in this situation to seek counseling, because the events of life have made them grow apart.

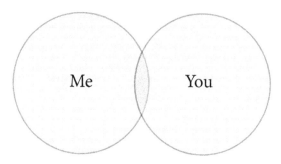

However, the excessive overlap of the individual circles also poses a threat to health in a marriage. Couples may feel this way when they do not have friendships outside of the marriage, or lack a sense of who they are as individuals. Although in this chapter we have mostly discussed the importance of expanding the "we" component, for a marriage to be truly healthy and growing in depth, each spouse must be on a journey of growth, health, and discovery in their own lives.

You are likely familiar with the common practice in wedding ceremonies of the unity candle in which one candle representing the bride and one candle representing the groom are used to light a larger, central candle representing the life they are starting as one. The original candles representing the bride and groom are often blown out. This metaphor conveys one aspect of the marriage partners joining together, but falls short in depicting the necessary continuation of the two original candles in order for the "we" candle to thrive.

It is essential for each partner to be able to sense that they continue to be their unique selves in the context of the relationship. With individual authenticity as the basis of togetherness, there cannot be unhealthy dependency or a "losing" of oneself for the other, nor a dominance of one person over the other. Each person's unique identity and personality is expressed and valued. Mutuality is the essential value of oneself *and* the other in a relationship. There are two people who are each unique and bring value to the shared relationship. This means there must also be boundaries and an awareness of where one person stops and the other begins. Interestingly, closeness with another person also requires closeness with oneself. To be connected to one's own needs and have self-compassion is not selfish, but centered and self-aware, and is the basis for loving the other.

For sustained, meaningful friendship, each person must be able to attend to personal needs and concerns. Each person must also respect the other's need to grow as a separate person. We do not need to question or know everything about the other person, and we need to allow and support their personal growth even as it occurs separately from our own. Having the ability to enact boundaries allows for more fully engaged intimacy. The following are questions to consider your personal authenticity within a relationship:

- Am I free to be really me?
- Is my voice valued in our discussions?
- Do I welcome my partner's voice as much as I push my own?
- Do I have a sense of how my partner and I are different and unique?
- Am I free to be with my own thoughts and feelings and to have them be my own?
- Can I let my spouse have his or her own personal convictions, feelings, joy, and pain?
- Do I feel able to pursue my own interests, and let my spouse do the same?
- Can we each do this in a way which does not distract from our shared goals and values, but helps us feel like healthy individuals?

Because the relationship is made up of "you" and "me," each person's health also impacts the health of the relationship. Like a recipe, if one of the ingredients is fermenting, the final product may still be edible, but the chances are it will taste a bit "off." In marriage, if the "me" circle is not healthy, it will contribute to the "us" part being a bit "off." Both our strengths and our brokenness will be present in the relationship. For each person to be able to contribute healthily to the relationship, it is important that each works on their own healing and growth, including sometimes reaching out for individual professional counseling.

SHARED MEANING AND PURPOSE

Why are we together? Do we have a common vision that unites us? What gives our relationship meaning? Some readers might assume that Christian faith answers the question of meaning. After all, marriage is a sacrament in the church, something which reflects the relational design of the Creator, and that is the end of the discussion.

But alas, simply *believing* in a specific purpose of marriage doesn't always sutain the *experience* of a meaningful marriage. God made us to be relational beings; we are built for dynamic, two-way conversation with God. So, instead of taking for granted the meaning of marriage, we—in the context of our individual lives and our marriage—are able to listen and discern what we feel called to, and what we are about. Instead of waiting for God to tell us the ultimate answers, we affirm God-given meaning in our lives by sensing our calling and making choices to say "yes" to that calling. Some questions that may help you explore the horizon of meaning and spiritual purpose in your marriage include:

- What are we (am I) here for?
- What gives our marriage (or my life) meaning?
- What are we becoming as a couple?
- What do we want to become as a couple?

- How do we intentionally work toward what we want to become?
- To what greater context (faith, family, culture) do we belong?
- How would we like to be remembered as a couple?
- What steps do we take to give back to our community or to the body of Christ?
- What are our gifts, together and as individuals?
- Where do we feel needed?

For Christian couples, you can prayerfully seek with openness and curiosity what God has for you as individuals and as a couple. It is important to have a sense of vision, individually and as a couple. We also affirm a deep bond with our partner not only through our shared sense of meaning, but by supporting each other's individual life goals. It is important that each person's sense of calling is taken seriously, and that each partner is supported in his or her "life goals." Against the backdrop of the "traditional" nuclear family of the 1950s (where men's success was supported by women at home), we may make gender-based assumptions about what *should* be meaningful for each person in a marriage partnership.

Don't let these assumptions limit your vision of marriage. Maybe a wife has a strong sense of God's working in her life through her public vocation and a husband has a strong sense of God's calling in raising the couple's children. Affirm and celebrate her vocation and financial provision for the family; celebrate and affirm that he is the one who is packing school lunches, attending parent-teacher conferences, going to children's medical appointments, reading stories with a toddler, or taking a teen for driving practice. Meaningful and equitable collaboration between men and women in ministry and public life must be supported by men and women working together with shared leadership at home.

In this discussion, you may have noticed that, aside from discussing domestic equality, we haven't yet mentioned children. For couples who have children, the gift and legacy of raising them can be meaningfully bonding. However, it is equally observable that the presence of children can also be divisive to the emotional bond between marriage partners. The urgency and stress of raising children and sometimes blending families can also pull couples apart. Raising children can connect a couple, but what happens when the children leave? If there is no shared meaning apart from children, the "empty nest" relationship is at risk. We encourage couples to be reflective and intentional in parenting, but they also need to cultivate dreams and visions as a couple, and to have time without the kids and without talking about the kids.

CHALLENGES TO THE JOURNEY OF FRIENDSHIP

Love, the emotional bond between partners, is powerful and mysterious. Author Sue Johnson summarizes, "The consensus across human history is that romantic love is, and always will be, an enigma, somehow by its very nature, unknowable."[7] Yet love draws us in. Despite its mystery, and despite its power to destroy, people still fall in love and build lives together around this emotional bond. The journey of friendship and intimacy in marriage is challenging. One of the challenges to marriage is a relationship with a power imbalance.

A relationship characterized by one partner wielding power over the other is fundamentally vulnerable to destruction; destruction of the individuals as well as the relationship itself. With a dynamic of power-*over*, the essential basis of mutuality is lost. Yet, too often, gender-based scripts within the church and in popular culture, are characterized by dominance and unilateral submission rather than authenticity and mutual submission. This distorts the "we" relationship in a marriage because it silences the God-given voice and power of one person in the marriage bond.

There has been a long history of teaching about Christian leadership—in the home and in the church—using the language of "headship." This concept is addressed elsewhere in this book, but here, we consider the psychological and relational consequences of unilateral headship. When one person takes on more power, they limit the other person's power and value within the marriage. Each person in a marriage deserves to feel that they are safe and treasured. Each person needs the opportunity to flourish, as opposed to feeling limited, devalued, or silenced. The person who takes on more power over the other also suffers, but in a different way. The person who takes on more power lacks the experience of mutual partnership with shared vulnerability.

HANDLING DIFFERENCES AND ROLES

As couples navigate entwining their lives in marriage, they need to discern how to handle decisions and tasks practically. How does the concept of mutuality help couples learn to handle the daily activities of filing taxes, eating meals, working jobs, taking out the garbage, cleaning the house, paying bills, and raising children? For these practical challenges, we encourage couples to talk openly about their goals and priorities and to make "who does what" decisions based on giftedness and availability, and for the common good of the couple, rather than on gender-based role expectations.

It is also important to recognize that there are changes throughout the seasons of a couple's life together, and if each person can maintain a "we" picture, flexibility and openness can be maintained. Couples must consider what is valuable to each person, to the couple, and to the family as a whole, and what is most needed now as well as the bigger picture. Learn to look for each other's needs, giftedness, and what each person enjoys and is good at. Take turns, shift roles, experiment, be open, and be practical. If you find what you are doing works well and each person finds fulfillment in it, rejoice. When something is "off," practice flexibility.

DEMANDS OUTSIDE OF THE FAMILY

A challenge for couples negotiating strengths, needs, and role responsibilities is that many aspects of society are not set up for egalitarian families. The single (male) breadwinner work week underlies many assumptions in workplace expectations. Sharing parenting and family responsibility is a challenge for men and women who are employed. Employees who ask for flexible timing at work in order to attend to parenting responsibilities are often judged according to the—increasingly uncommon— standard of a family with a separate breadwinner and homemaker. Deciding roles and responsibilities both at home and outside the home is an important and creative challenge for working men and women.

Being a part of a community can also be a way to live out God's calling for your marriage. As a sacrament, marriage is a visible display of God's intimacy and love for us, and simply being a loving and thriving Christian couple in the world can fulfill God's calling for your marriage. Said another way, living a normal life together (taking children to soccer practices, resolving endless scheduling conflicts, and dividing up holidays between families) in an honoring, mutually supportive, and respectful way can actually be a form of ministry. Having a deep and fulfilling marriage bond is not exclusive of regular life and family activities; it is possible to love and be loved well, within the context of a life with pressures and challenges.

Raising Children

We recognize that children are a big part of marriage and, as discussed earlier, can be a gift for, as well as a threat to, a couple's journey of friendship and intimacy. Within the limited scope of this chapter's focus, we would like to highlight the concept of mutuality and power-with as characterizing the parenting relationship of an egalitarian marriage. Children come into our lives as their own persons, whether adopted or biological, or blended through marriage. Each child is different and children cannot be understood on the basis of who their parents are. In spite of the moral and legal responsibilities of raising children, we do not own our children. They are their own persons with their own capacity for free agency in this world. When a marriage is based in mutual self-giving love, the parents in this marriage have a strong basis to recognize that the God-given value and full personhood of their child is not created or owned by the parents. The question, "What does this child need?" needs to be asked uniquely for each child you parent in each circumstance the child experiences.

We encourage parents to receive their children with hospitality as divine gifts. Perhaps it is a strange idea to suggest that parents offer hospitality to their own child in the first home that the child ever knows. Does this imply that the parents' home is not the child's home? What we mean by hospitality is that the relationship from the parents to the child acknowledges the separate personhood of the child. As Henri Nouwen stated, "children are not properties to own and rule over, but gifts to cherish and care for. Our children are our most important guests, who enter into our home, ask for careful attention, stay for a while and then leave to follow their own way."[8]

In a way, a child enters our life as a stranger—a beloved stranger to which we come to feel attached, bonded, and committed to, and who we learn to love deeply. Sometimes parents are so blinded by the focus of "training" a child that they miss out on seeing their unique child. Children have their own moral and spiritual agency to do good and to do evil. They have their own needs, styles, preferences, loves, strengths, vulnerabilities, and giftedness. A parent can never know what their child will become tomorrow; they can only receive the child and his or her unique needs, strengths, and limitations, today. We encourage you to receive your children as treasures and mysteries who need space and safe boundaries to become themselves through your love and hospitality.

CONCLUDING THOUGHTS, QUESTIONS FOR REFLECTION, AND EXERCISES FOR COUPLES

Saying "I do" to love and commitment is a mystery. Getting married is not a simple path toward happiness, but it can be a fulfilling path of sanctification. In marriage, we learn how to give space and to take up space, and how to have an authentic voice without dominating over the other's voice. In the sustained commitment to this relationship of love where "fully me" and "fully you" journey in "we," marriage is a way to know God.

In love, there is suffering and conflict. Navigating suffering, conflict, and betrayals of trust requires that we learn to hold our own pride carefully. Sometimes, it is more important to work together than to be right. Neither partner holds the whole truth. Suffering can yield fruit, and recognizing that holiness is a greater goal than immediate satisfaction can help sustain couples. On this journey, marriage partners remain friends when they hold each other's safety, give each other time and attention, respect each other's authenticity, and share a vision for their relationship. Wherever you are in your journey of marriage, we leave you with our wish that you find grace, healing, and growth in your lives together.

QUESTIONS FOR REFLECTION FOR INDIVIDUALS OR COUPLES/GROUPS

- What was particularly charming and inspiring about my partner at the beginning of our relationship?
- What has my encounter with my partner brought out in me?
- What were/are our strengths and special capacities as a couple?
- What have been/are our greatest challenges in relating to each other?
- How do we know if our relationship is thriving, or if it needs special care and attention?
- Looking back, what are the signs we may have missed along the way that our relationship wasn't getting what it needed in order to survive?
- Do we have a common vision? How can we allow ourselves to find it?
- How can I invite or let my partner help me spread the wings of my soul? How can I help my partner spread the wings of his/her soul? What are the next steps towards this, individually and as a couple?

EXPERIENTIAL EXERCISES

The following activities are designed for couples to cultivate meaningful conversations and connections.

Use Images for Visioning and Reflecting. Take turns selecting a photo of your own, or something you've found, that represents your experience of your marriage. Ask yourself what the image means, and why it means that to you. What embodies you as a couple? What has resonance for you? Let the picture teach you, and let your heart speak and answer. Then share these photos or images with each other. Take turns explaining why you chose the photo that you did. Ask questions of the other person's choice. Then, with curiosity and graciousness, try to select a photo, or a few, that represent your vision for your marriage as a couple. This might represent an integration of your two different photos, or could even be a collage of images that demonstrate your shared vision. Feel free to pick words and symbols along the way that help you craft what you want that vision to be.

Re-Create Old Dates. Find time to do something you used to do when you first started your relationship, which you haven't done recently. This might mean going back to a favorite restaurant or visiting a spot in nature where you had an early date. If you live far away from where you used to, recreate a date or even a meal you enjoyed together. Take time to talk about how you saw each other then, and what you loved about each other then. Share stories of when you first knew you loved the other person, and what attracted you to them.

Make a point of telling the other person how you have seen them grow as a person since then, and what you know and love about them now that you have been together longer.

Build Love Maps.[9] Love maps represent knowledge about your partner's life that creates a strong foundation for friendship and intimacy. Couples who are close know each other's worlds. This knowledge is like a map where you keep track of important events in your partner's history, which is updated continuously as you share your lives together. Extensive knowledge of your partner helps to build a foundation for friendship and intimacy and resources to deal with stress and change. Be aware going into the exercise that you won't be able to answer every question correctly. This adds an element of playfulness as you intentionally try to discover more about each other's experiences. What follows are some questions for you and your partner to try answering about each other to get you started.* Feel free to add your own questions.

- Name my two closest friends.
- What stresses am I facing right now?
- What is my fondest unrealized dream?
- What is one of my greatest fears or disaster scenarios?
- What is my favorite way to spend an evening?
- What is one of my favorite ways to be soothed?

*These questions are downloaded and adapted from the website of the Gottman Institute (https://www.gottman.com/blog/the-sound-relationship-house-build-love-maps/) where more exercises are available to strengthen couples' relationships.

- What are some of the important events coming up in my life? How do I feel about them?
- What do I worry most about?
- What was my most embarrassing moment?

Recovering Pathways to Connection. Take turns telling each other about a time when you felt close and intimate. This may include physical intimacy, but focus in particular on emotional intimacy, and when your hearts felt connected. When your spouse tells you about when they felt close to you, ask questions to learn more. What was unique about that for you? Why do you think that touched you so deeply? What did you know about yourself, about me, or about us, when that happened? What are ways that we can cultivate that closeness in our life now?

Conversations for a Couple. Set time aside, with no distractions, to ask each other the following questions. If you're able, make this time special in some way, and something to look forward to. You may want to take notes to remember what your partner says.

- What did we do well at the beginning of our relationship that contributed to health in the "us" part of our relationship?
- What got in the way of those things happening?
- What would be meaningful for us to start doing again?

These can be things that happened at the beginning of the relationship like buying flowers, dressing up to go on dates, etc. Be good students of each other, learning and taking stock of what the other person has told you. Then most importantly, make a commitment in your heart and to each other to do those things. After the conversation, take time to reflect. If it works for you, write a brief letter to your spouse about what you learned from the conversation, what you love about the other person, and what your renewed commitment is to them. For other couples, it might suffice to have a list posted on the fridge or on the calendar about your intentions to do what you did at first.

Recommended for Further Reading

Daring Greatly: How the Courage to be Vulnerable Transforms the Way we Live, Love, Parent, and Lead by Brene Brown. New York: Avery, 2012

The Science of Trust: Emotional Attunement for Couples by John Gottman. New York: Norton, 2011.

The Seven Principles for Making Marriage Work by John Gottman and Nan Silver. New York: Harmony Books, 2015.

Hold me Tight: Seven Conversations for a Lifetime of Love by Sue Johnson. New York: Little Brown and Company, 2008.

Love Sense: The Revolutionary New Science of Romantic Relationships by Sue Johnson. New York: Little Brown and

Company, 2013.

Forever And Always: The Art of Intimacy by Steven Tracy and Celestia Tracy. Eugene: Wipf and Stock, 2011.

– 3 –

Communicating as a Couple

Lynne Nelson

You might be familiar with statements like these:

> "We never agree on anything!"
> "You always get your own way!"
> "I'm sick and tired of this arguing!"

Do you recognize any of these exclamations? Are you wondering if you can make improvements to communication in your marriage? Even if you feel you already communicate effectively, you can still learn tools to strengthen your relationship. Improved communication can grow your feelings of love and affection for each other.

In Genesis, God establishes that the man and woman will develop connection and closeness with each other in marriage. We read, "...a man leaves his father and mother and is joined to his wife, and the two are united into one" (Gen. 2:24 NLT). Jesus emphasized this unity stating that the "one flesh" in a marriage relationship be respected. "Since they are no longer two but one, let no one split apart what God has joined together" (Matt. 19:6 NLT).

In my practice, I often hear couples say, "We just don't communicate well with each other." That might mean that they fight, yell, call each other insulting names, and don't resolve disagreements. Or it can mean that one partner is silent and the spouse does not know what they are thinking or feeling. Learning techniques for effective communication with your spouse will guide you toward developing the unity that God intends and will deepen your appreciation for each other.

WHY DO WE NEED TO STUDY COMMUNICATION?

You might ask, "Why can't I just be my natural self? … I want to speak my mind when and where I feel like it… I want to be me… Anything else sounds unnatural and stifling." Or perhaps you do not see the need to learn about communication. But happy marriages do not just happen automatically. Consider that fifty percent of married couples divorce and many of those who stay together are unhappy.[1] Expressing your unfiltered reactions does not work to bring mutual care and respect into your relationship. Rather, using kind and effective communication patterns is essential to build and maintain that best friend relationship with your spouse. When both partners create and maintain an atmosphere of safety, you are then able to express vulnerability and show your authentic selves.

God calls us to be equipped. "Get all the advice and instruction you can, so you will be wise the rest of your life" (Prov. 19:20 NLT). You are equipping yourselves as you learn skilled communication patterns. Where do we learn healthy communication skills? We do not come into life with innate wisdom on how to achieve this kind of communication[We may not grow up seeing effective communication modeled for us. However, just as we study to prepare for careers or other life pursuits, we can learn and develop communication skills with respect and integrity that enable us to honor our marriage vows.]

TWO-WAY COMMUNICATION

Two-way communication is a distinct feature in a marriage that is based on equality and mutuality. This style empowers both spouses to actively express themselves with the minds and hearts that God gave them. In two-way communication, both people strive to understand each other and to respond to each other with regard and esteem. This calls for you to take into account each person's views, needs, and desires. This does not require eloquence, but it does require that you both speak with clarity, grace, and kindness, and that you take the time to empathize with the other's perspective.

In a marriage, each person brings their own set of ideas, dreams, and abilities. These different perspectives set up a situation where conflict can arise. Because there are two distinct people involved, we can think of conflict as a regular— even normal—part of a healthy relationship. If it seems that there are no differences between you and your spouse, then it is likely that one person is dominant and the other is not acknowledging his or her feelings, needs, and desires. When conflict exists, it needs to be addressed, and if it is not addressed in a way that honors each person, it leads to a loss of passion and love, resulting in emotional and/or physical separation, and an obvious loss of unity.

USING COMMUNICATION TO KNOW, UNDERSTAND, AND EMPATHIZE WITH EACH OTHER

There are two sides to interpersonal communication: listening and speaking. The listening side of communication is as important as the speaking side of communication. The Bible encourages us to listen carefully to each other. "Spouting off before listening to the facts is both shameful and foolish" (Prov. 18:13 NLT). "Understand this, my dear brothers and sisters: you must all be quick to listen, slow to speak, and slow to get angry" (James 1:19 NLT). It is not possible for two people to communicate if both are merely speaking to the air. The significance of listening to understand is expressed by Rob Lees:

> When people are seeking to understand, it is as if two sets of eyes are fixed on the one soul. Both parties in the relationship focus on what one of them is attempting to communicate...they have to take time to arrive at the meaning behind the words. It has been my experience that the process of understanding is one of the closest things I can think of to a "cure-all" in relationships... Understanding itself builds a closeness that allows relationships to grow.[2]

Empathy grows as you listen to your spouse and focus on being fully with them. You show care by being there and listening, sensing their feelings and needs. Marshall Rosenberg captures this kind of empathy by saying, "What is essential is our ability to be present to what's really going on within—to the unique feelings and needs a person is experiencing in that very moment."[3]

Conversations vary in their significance and the degree of impact on the people involved. You can choose the style of your discussion according to its importance. The more significant an issue appears to be, then the more careful and structured you need to be in your style of conversation.

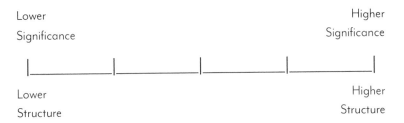

There are specific techniques to help you to listen and to speak effectively. In this next exercise, on working through conflict, each person takes a turn as speaker and as listener.[4] Intentionally taking turns is important in the process of working on solutions or compromises. The following chart includes concepts from the Gottman Institute and from my own experience of aiding couples.

Kind and attentive listening allows the other person to feel safe and to honestly express him or herself. Acknowledging the other's view does not imply that you like, or agree with, what the other is expressing, but demonstrates you are seeking to know and understand them more fully. After you both reach understanding, you can then brainstorm ideas toward resolving your difficulties.

Points for the Listener and the Speaker

Listener Jobs	Speaker Jobs
Postpone your own agenda.	Speak clearly.
Focus on the speaker.	Take time to think.
Help the speaker feel safe from your judgment or opinion.	Go deep inside for your thoughts and emotions.
Listen in order to understand. Problem solve later.	Express your feelings in words.
Listen for emotions.	Use "I" statements.
Create open body posture: look at the speaker, don't cross your arms, scowl, or shake your head "no."	Do not blame or criticize. Avoid accusing "you" statements.
Validate the speaker (nod, a kind expression, 'mm-hmm'). This does not mean agreement, but that you are listening.	Share your perspective.
Allow pauses or tears. Do not interrupt.	Get to know yourself better as you talk.
Wait for a pause. You may ask curious questions, paraphrase, or ask for clarification.	State your need or longing.

ASKING GOOD QUESTIONS

The way you ask a question can either open up and expand a conversation or limit that conversation and keep it small. There are three different kinds of questions and each brings its own result.

Closed Questions. A closed question can be answered with one word. For example, "How was your day?" "Fine." "Do you like the soup?" "Yeah." "What color is the paint?" "Blue." A closed question can result in a fairly meaningless one-word reply, or it can cut the other person off. It does not open the door for further and deeper discussion.

Curious Questions. The curious question is open-ended, thus it is a conversation door opener. It cannot be answered with one word. It invites further discussion and expression. It is not judgmental. It shows that the questioner is interested in the mind and heart of the other person. Curious questions increase learning about the other person and their perspective. One curious question can lead to another curious question while at the same time each person's response expands the conversation. A conversation going back and forth like this can be a lot of fun.

Here are some examples of *curious questions*:

> Could you tell me more about ...?
> What parts of ... are most important to you?
> Can you share with me your goal in this area?

A conversation is a discussion between people sharing thoughts, feelings, and information. One statement leads to another, related comment. The words go back and forth like people bouncing a ball back and forth. Curious questions facilitate this kind of conversation.

The opposite of such a conversation is a monologue in which one person blurts out information without relating it to the input of the other person. A person engaging in this way might wrongly think that they are communicating just by keeping words flowing. It is as if silence or reflection is frightening, or perhaps the speaker is simply not interested in the other person. The people in this so-called conversation are not responding to or interacting with each other. Monologue is not two-way communication.

Why Questions. If you are seeking to broaden a conversation, a why question is discouraged. Examples of why questions include, "Why are you so upset?" "Why didn't you finish that?" "Why don't you ever listen?" Why questions immediately imply a disagreement with or disapproval of the other person. These are often accusative and may set up an argument in which each person develops an agenda to prove they are right.

Four Styles of Communication to Avoid

How we speak and what we say can be a power for good in a relationship or for the demise of the relationship. "The tongue can bring death or life; those who love to talk will reap the consequences" (Prov. 18:21 NLT). As you consider how to use your words in a positive way, "Let your conversation be always full of grace, seasoned with salt, so that you may know how to answer everyone" (Col. 4:6 NIV).

In his book, *The Seven Principles for Making Marriage Work*, Dr. John Gottman identifies four communication patterns to avoid, which he calls the Four Horsemen of the Apocalypse.[5] These four styles of interaction correlate with the destruction of relationships.[6] In the illustration below,[7] the Four Horsemen patterns to avoid are in the left column, and the methods to use instead of the four negative patterns, or antidotes, are in the right column.

Stop the Four Horsemen with their Antidotes

CRITICISM → Use Gentle Start Up

DEFENSIVENESS → Take Responsibility

CONTEMPT → Describe Your Own Feelings and Needs
Don't Describe Your Partner

STONEWALLING → Do Physiological Self-Soothing

The discussion below considers each of the "four horsemen" and their antidotes.[8] What you say makes a big difference. You have power in your words, and should avoid antagonizing each other. Proverbs says, "Starting a quarrel is like opening a floodgate, so stop before a dispute breaks out" (Prov. 17:14 NLT). Learning positive communication tools can help you escape from many serious arguments and wounds.

CRITICISM

The word criticism means a broad sweeping attack on the character of the other person. Criticism blames your partner for problems. Criticism implies that the other person is flawed, wrong, or bad, and can incite a defensive response from them. Critical statements include things like, "How can you be so foolish?", or "You have a ridiculous idea!"

A criticism is distinct from a complaint. A complaint is a description of something you don't like and wish to see changed. Complaints, when spoken graciously, are a necessary part of bringing change and maintaining harmony within a relationship. A complaint is about your wishes regarding a specific action. Criticism is an accusation about the character of your partner.

ANTIDOTE TO CRITICISM: MAKE A CLEAR POLITE COMPLAINT

You want to speak truthfully, without blaming or insulting your spouse. To accomplish this you need to speak kindly yet specifically with an "I Statement." The "I Statement" involves a three step process:

- You *describe the situation* you are challenged with.
- You put your *emotions into words*. Tell your partner how you feel. Use words to name your emotions such as sad, frustrated, anxious, disappointed, overwhelmed, etc.
- You *request* the behavior you desire in your spouse.

When making your "I Statement," be careful to describe only yourself and your experience. Just speak about the situation at hand, how you feel, and request a specific desired outcome. You do not want to describe or blame your partner as in a statement like, "I feel you did a poor job." When you state your feelings, you invite your spouse to enter into your emotional world. Since feelings are felt and owned by each of us personally, your partner cannot legitimately negate you by saying, "No you don't feel that way," or "You shouldn't feel that way."

DEFENSIVENESS

Defensiveness is when you counter back to your partner's complaint or criticism. It is a self-protective move, in which you pose yourself as the victim, and try to make yourself sound more right. Or, defensiveness might be repeatedly saying how well you are behaving, while still avoiding the current issue. Defensive statements are an underhanded way to blame your partner and divert from the issue in question. Defensiveness doesn't solve anything, but it does escalate the problem at hand.

ANTIDOTE TO DEFENSIVENESS: TAKE RESPONSIBILITY

The way to avoid defensiveness is to take responsibility for your part in the matter. For example, consider that Mary says she is upset by Joe's clutter on the table at dinnertime. If Joe were to accept responsibility for the clutter and say, "Oh, I can pick up my stuff before dinnertime," then the matter would be solved. Instead, if Joe were to say, "Doesn't anybody appreciate me around here?" or, "Just look at your stuff on the couch!" he would not be taking responsibility for his part, and then their issue grows bigger. Other helpful responses to one partner's complaint could be questions that seek understanding like: "What is it that you need?" or "What are you concerned about?" or "How can I help?"

CONTEMPT

Contempt is when one person speaks with a sense of superiority, putting themselves above their partner. The person speaks from a position of being better than the other. It may involve insults, name calling, hostile humor, or globalizing phrases like "You never ..." or "You always ..." Contempt is particularly hurtful in a relationship.

ANTIDOTE TO CONTEMPT: RECOGNIZE THE GOOD IN YOUR PARTNER

Scripture urges us to have positive regard for others. That should be especially true for our partners. We read "Be devoted to each other with mutual affection. Excel at showing respect for each other" (Rom. 12:10 ISV). Therefore, the antidote to contempt is to treat each other with respect and proactively work on recognizing and speaking of the good traits in your partner. Because contempt is deadly to your relationship, remember to speak words of kindness and appreciation to your partner.

One very practical means to build up your spouse is to *intentionally respond* whenever he or she speaks directly to you. If you respond ...

- With silence: your spouse knows you chose to ignore them; this makes him or her feel unimportant.
- With indifference: your spouse realizes you heard, but simply aren't very interested.
- With interest: the relationship builds and a conversation may follow.

STONEWALLING

When a listener withdraws from the conversation without resolving any issues, that person is stonewalling.

There are various ways to stonewall including: shutting down engagement with the conversation, changing the subject, turning away, or physically leaving. The conversation may begin with a harsh expression of criticism or contempt, then comes defensiveness, and finally one partner tunes out, or stonewalls. Of course, the conversation goes nowhere after this point.

Research reveals that the person who stonewalls is being plagued by physiological arousal as in a heart rate of over 100 beats per minute.[9] When this happens, the person's brain cannot engage with its usual capacity and ability.

This person needs to ask for a break from the conversation so they can calm down before continuing.

ANTIDOTE TO STONEWALLING: GIVE YOUR MIND A BREAK

Notice how the writer of Proverbs directs us to wisely consider our ways: "The prudent understand where they are going, but fools deceive themselves" (Prov. 14:8 NLT). We need to be wise in our conversation. When you feel too physically and/or emotionally intense to continue a conversation, you need to take a break so that you can return later and have a constructive interaction. The antidote to stonewalling is to take a time out and together agree when to return to the conversation. A mental break brings relief to your mind. The Three B's below offer ways to calm your body and your brain and allow you to return to the conversation.

BREATHE - BURN ENERGY - BREAK

- Breathing: slow and deep breathing (move your diaphragm not your chest).
- Burn Energy: walking, running, jumping jacks, bicycling, etc.
- Break: change your mental activity by reading or doing another project.

When you take a break with the intention of returning to the conversation, you are not stonewalling, you are preparing to enter the conversation again with renewed readiness. You are giving thought to your ways in a wise manner. Use one of the Three B's for at least 20 minutes during your time out. Intentionally return to your conversation at the appointed time.

COMMUNICATION IN DECISION-MAKING

William D. Spencer and Aída B. Spencer offer a beautiful model of egalitarian communication and decision-making within a pattern of shared power.[10] Their methods honor each person in the relationship as an equal; each created with personal abilities, wishes, needs, and ideas.

The Spencers describe their marriage as one of mutual submission in which "two ruling authorities [are] bowing or submitting to each other because they bow to a greater authority: Christ the Lord."[11] Each person leads out of his or her area of talents and preparedness; their roles are not based on their gender. They see that God commissioned both Adam and Eve (male and female) to rule, serve, protect, and work the earth (Genesis 1:26-28). In their shared leadership, when faced with a large personal decision of high significance, the Spencers enter decision-making with careful communication processes:

1. Engage in prayer.
2. Obtain information and counsel.
3. Write out the negative and the positive aspects.
4. Gather more information as needed.
5. Pray again.[12]

They then ask the following types of questions to focus their decision-making:

- What would do more to advance God's kingdom?
- How does this new possibility fit with each of our ministry models and our particular spiritual gifts?
- Can someone else do this better?
- How would each choice affect each member of our family?
- What will this cost our family? Is it a higher benefit than we can give?

For important matters they always make a joint decision. One person never makes a final decision on important matters that affect the other.[13]

✳ COMMUNICATING IN PROBLEM SOLVING

The goal of problem solving is to get to a "yes" that affirms both people in the relationship. One way to do this is by using "The Art of Compromise." This tool is designed to help you explore each of your views and desires on an issue. Each of you takes time to consider what areas you feel you have some flexibility on, and what areas you see as inflexible. Keep your inflexible areas as few as possible and your flexible areas as broad as possible. This exercise is most useful after you have extensively shared your perspectives with each other by taking turns in both the speaking and listening role.

THE ART OF COMPROMISE[14]

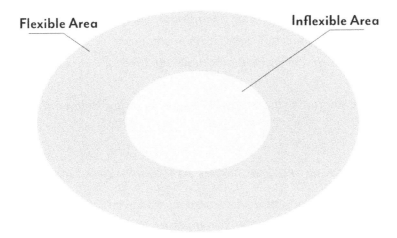

Flexible Area

Inflexible Area

My inflexible area or core need on this issue is:

My more flexible areas on this issue are:

YIELD TO WIN: COMPROMISE WITH ME LIKE I AM SOMEONE YOU LOVE.

Getting to "Yes." Discuss these questions with your partner
- Help me understand why your inflexible area is so important to you.
- What are your core feelings, beliefs, or values about this issue?
- Help me understand your flexible areas.

- What do we agree about?
- How might these goals be accomplished?
- How can we reach a temporary compromise?
- What feelings do we have in common?
- How can I help to meet your core needs?

Our compromise that honors both our needs and dreams is:

COMMUNICATING IN THE AFTERMATH OF A FIGHT

Couples will inevitably have areas of disagreement, and not all conflicts are about right and wrong issues or actions. Some are due to the differing styles and preferences of each person, and both people may play a role in the conflict. As you are able to discuss and resolve such differences with each other in the journey of your friendship, you can deepen your connection, understand the views and needs of each other, maintain better rapport, and therefore, help prevent some bigger injuries from happening in the future.

Being able to speak of your own experience honestly, and also listening to the other's perspective, is a part of this process. The Gottman Institute has developed an exercise to help couples to process and evaluate what happened in an argument (the exercise is presented on the next page).

As you proceed in the guided step-by-step process, you each speak for yourself and you also hear and validate your partner's view. You are led to the point of making your own apology and hearing the apology of your partner. Then you each have the choice to accept the other's apology or state what you need further from your spouse. A five-minute argument may take up to an hour to process. The investment of time results in an increased comfort level, and the ability to work with and trust in your partner.

AFTERMATH OF A FIGHT OR REGRETTABLE INCIDENT COUPLE EXERCISE[15]

This exercise is for "processing" past fights, regrettable incidents, or past emotional injuries. "Processing" means that you can talk about the incident without getting back into it again. It needs to be a conversation—as if you were both sitting in the balcony of a theater looking down on the stage where the action had occurred. This requires *calm* and some emotional distance from the incident.

Before you begin, keep in mind the goal is greater understanding—addressing the process and how the issue was talked about—without getting back into the fight. So, wait until you're both calm.

We assume that each of your realities has validity. Perception is everything. Don't focus on "the facts." Pay attention to the common barriers to communication and their antidotes as you move through the process. Keeping the "Four Horsemen" diagram handy can help.

STEP ONE: FEELINGS.
Share how you felt, without saying why you felt that way. Avoid commenting on your partner's feelings (Suggestions can be found on the next page).

I felt...

defensive

not listened to

feelings got hurt

totally flooded

angry

sad

unloved

misunderstood

criticized

took a complaint personally

like you didn't even like me

not cared about

worried

afraid

unsafe

tense

I was right and you were wrong

both of us were partly right

out of control

frustrated

righteously indignant

morally justified

unfairly picked on

unappreciated

disliked

unattractive

stupid

morally outraged

taken for granted

like leaving

like staying and talking this through

I was overwhelmed with emotion

not calm

stubborn

powerless

I had no influence

I wanted to win this one

my opinions didn't even matter

there was a lot of give and take

I had no feelings at all

I had no idea what I was feeling

lonely

alienated

ashamed

guilty

culpable

abandoned

disloyal

exhausted

foolish

remorseful

shocked

Step Two: Realities.

Describe your "reality." Take turns. Summarize and validate at least a part of your partner's reality.

Subjective Reality and Validation

1. Take turns describing your perceptions, your own reality of what happened during the regrettable incident. Describe yourself. Don't describe your partner. Avoid attack and blame. Talk about what you might have needed from your partner. Describe your perceptions like a reporter, giving an objective blow-by-blow description. Say "I heard you saying," rather than "You said."

2. Summarize and then validate your partner's reality by saying something like, "It makes sense to me how you saw this and what your perceptions and needs were. I get it." Use empathy by saying something like, "I can see why this upset you." Validation doesn't mean you agree, but that you can understand even a part of your partner's experience of the incident.

3. Do both partners feel understood? If yes, move on. If no, ask, "What do I need to know to understand your perspective better?" Afterward, ask your partner, "Did I get it?" and "Is there anything else?"

Step Three: Triggers.

Share what experiences or memories you've had that might have escalated the interaction, and the stories of why these are triggers for each of you.

As you rewind the video tape of your memory, stop at a point where you had a similar set of feelings triggered in the past. Now tell the story of that past moment to your partner, so your partner can understand why that is a trigger for you.

Share your stories—it will help your partner understand you. As you think about your early history or childhood, is there a story you remember that relates to what got triggered in you, your "enduring vulnerabilities?" Your partner needs to know you, so that they can be more sensitive to you.

Examples of triggers:

I felt judged. *I'm very sensitive to that.*

I felt excluded. *I'm very sensitive to that.*

I felt criticized. *I'm very sensitive to that.*

I felt flooded.

I felt ashamed.

I felt lonely.

I felt belittled.

I felt disrespected.

I felt powerless.

I felt out of control.

Other

Validation: Does any part of your partner's triggers and story make sense to you?

Step Four: Responsibility.

Acknowledge your own role in contributing to the fight or regrettable incident. Recognize that under ideal conditions, you might have done better at talking about this issue.

1. What set me up for the miscommunication? Share how you set yourself up to get into this conflict. Read aloud the items that were true for you on the following list:

I've been very stressed and irritable lately .

I've not expressed much appreciation toward you lately.

I've taken you for granted.

I've been overly sensitive lately.

I've been overly critical lately.

I've not shared very much of my inner world.

I've not been emotionally available.

I've been turning away more.

I've been getting easily upset.

I've been depressed lately.

I've had a chip on my shoulder lately.

I've not been very affectionate.

I've not made time for good things between us.

I've not been a very good listener lately.

I've not asked for what I needed.

I've been feeling a bit like a martyr.

I've needed to be alone.

I've not wanted to take care of anybody.

I have been very preoccupied.

I haven't felt very much confidence in myself.

I've been running on empty.

2. What do you regret specifically, and what was your contribution to the incident?

3. What do you wish to apologize for? (Read aloud from examples on the next page)

I'm sorry that:

I over-reacted.   I was so negative.
I was really grumpy.   Other...
I was defensive.

4. If you accept your partner's apology, say so. If not, say what you still need.

Step Five: Constructive Plans.

Plan together one way that each of you can make it better next time. Share one thing your partner can do to make a discussion of this issue better next time. (It's important to remain calm as you do this.) Then, while it's still your turn, share one thing you can do to make it better next time. What do you need to be able to put this behind you and move on? Be as agreeable as possible to the plans suggested by your partner. Write your plan to make it better:

Conclusion

By implementing these communication patterns you as spouses will be more equipped to:

- create a safe place to enjoy life with each other and maintain your friendship.
- develop an intimate understanding and knowledge of each other.
- honor the deep, underlying yearnings in each other.

- manage your ongoing conflicts.
- resolve your solvable problems, face major conflict, and solve problems.
- model gracious and effective communication to your family and to others.

As you follow these patterns in communication, you will be living out scriptures that direct us to build each other up within the Body of Christ., "So encourage each other and build each other up, just as you are already doing (1 Thess. 5:11, NLT). Similarly Paul says, "So then, let us aim for harmony in the church and try to build each other up" (Rom. 14:9 NLT).

As you honor each other in marriage by using positive communication skills that encourage and lift each other up, you are deepening the unity of your relationship. The investment of time and energy in learning and growing in communication skills will bring satisfaction and peace as you interact with each other.

Questions for Discussion and Reflection

1. What positive style of communication do you already use as a couple?
2. What problematic communication styles do you tend to gravitate toward?
3. What are the elements of good listening?
4. Which of the practical suggestions do you think you could begin implementing right away?

RECOMMENDED FOR FURTHER READING

The Seven Principles for Making Marriage Work by John M. Gottman and Nan Silver. New York: Harmony, 2015.

Nonviolent Communication: A Language of Life, (3rd. Ed.) by Marshall B. Encinitas Rosenberg. CA: Puddle Dancer Press, 2015.

Fighting for Your Marriage: Positive Steps for Preventing Divorce and Preserving a Lasting Love by Howard Markman, Scott Stanley, and Susan L. Blumberg. San Francisco: Jossey-Bass Inc., Publishers, 1994.

– 4 –

Money Matters

David M. Nelson

Issues involving financial management are the cause of friction in many relationships. To many people, money is a painful subject. It stirs our emotions. It makes us mad, envious, happy, miserable, and sometimes a little hostile. A couple brings into their relationship patterns that they have observed from their parents, or if they have been single adults for a number of years, patterns that they have established themselves. These patterns can include very different views on spending versus saving, borrowing and buying on credit, charitable contributions, earning a living, and work-life balance decisions. This chapter offers guidance based on Scripture as to how a couple can work through important issues regarding family finances in an egalitarian relationship.

STEWARDSHIP AND OUR ATTITUDE ABOUT POSSESSIONS

In the first verse of the first chapter of the first book of the Bible we read, "In the beginning God created the heavens and the earth." (Gen. 1:1) and in the book of Psalms, the psalmist David says, "The earth is the Lord's, and everything in it, the world and all who live in it;" (Ps. 24:1). God has entrusted his entire creation to us, starting with man and woman in the marriage relationship in Genesis. He asks us to be good stewards of the creation. He has given us each different skills and abilities, different areas of influence, and control over certain resources.

In the New Testament, Jesus stresses the importance of being a faithful manager of what you have been entrusted in the parable of the talents (see Matt. 25:14-30). The parable also indicates that as we manage well what we have been given, we will be given more. Jesus even says that the way that we handle worldly wealth is a proving ground for being entrusted with true spiritual riches:

> Whoever can be trusted with very little can also be trusted with much, and whoever is dishonest with very little will also be dishonest with much. So if you have not been trustworthy in handling worldly wealth, who will trust you with true riches?(Luke 16:10–11)

Bringing Diverse Skills Together in Financial Decision-making

The basis for financial decision-making is to recognize that we are stewards of God's creation. This mutually shared attitude creates the foundation for all other decisions—such as working and earning, giving, spending, and saving. When we faithfully follow God's plan, he promises to meet all our needs "according to his glorious riches in Christ Jesus" (Phil. 4:19).

From the shared understanding of stewardship, each person in the relationship brings different abilities and strengths into financial management. One individual might have a much higher market wage or have a greater knowledge of saving and investment opportunities; another might know more about needs and giving opportunities, or might be more adept at handling the practical aspects of money management. Each couple needs to look at the skills that they each have and divide up functions in the financial area based on each individual's gifting and inclination. Where one party in a relationship has greater expertise than the other, open communication with honesty and transparency results in decisions made by mutual consent. While responsibilities may be divided up, the major financial priorities need to be jointly established. In addition, by understanding each other's strengths and abilities in financial decision-making, a couple can also identify areas where they might need to seek outside expertise.

Discuss

- In the area of financial management, what are each of your strengths?
- What experience, if any, do you bring to this area?
- Are there areas where neither of you has experience? How might you find the help you need?
- How can you complement each other in managing your resources?

Financial Management Components

The fundamental economic problem facing humankind is that of scarcity. The desires we have as human beings exceeds our resources so we need to make choices as to how to use those resources to best meet our needs and wants. Financial management decisions relate to obtaining the resources we need to meet the needs we have, managing those resources, and then deciding how to use those resources to meet our needs and those of others. Scripture provides insight into each of these areas.

EARNING A LIVING

God made work as an important part of life and is the primary means by which most of us will obtain the resources we need to meet our needs. Tending and caring for the garden of Eden was a task assigned by God before the fall and we are told that in heaven there will be work we will do. The Bible has numerous verses warning of slothfulness and the severe consequences of being lazy.

Proverbs 10:4 sums it up succinctly: "Lazy hands make for poverty, but diligent hands bring wealth." To honor God and each other, and to provide for the resources needed to meet our needs and those of others, it is important that we use our time well in performing productive activities. Using our time well means striking a balance between being diligent about the *work* we do to earn a living and the *living* we do as God's children. God established the principle of the Sabbath to give us a break from work. Just as we want to avoid being lazy and slothful, we want to avoid becoming workaholics.

Over the past couple of hundred years the world of work has experienced a dramatic transformation as advances in technology and the utilization of reliable cheap energy has put an increasing premium on brain power versus brute force. The wage gap between individuals with a high school education versus a college or graduate school education has widened over time. Employers want to hire individuals who know how to use today's technology, who are persons of integrity and honesty, who have good written and/or oral communication skills, who can work well with others, who take initiative and are diligent in their work effort, and who are good problem solvers. Obtaining the skills to be a desirable employee or to be successful in one's own business requires a substantial investment in education and training, usually at considerable sacrifice.

How does a couple in an egalitarian relationship approach questions related to life's vocation? A suggestion is to have each individual in the relationship work through the answers to the three questions represented by the circle diagram on the next page. Then discuss your thoughts and dreams with each other and pray for God's guidance. Work to develop a plan that will allow each of you as individuals and as a couple to realize the potential that God has for you. There are likely to be tradeoffs such as, "I'll work so you can finish nursing school and once you are employed I'll go back to school and get the training I need to become a teacher." In a marriage there should never be an attitude of superiority because of one partner's position or earnings. Much relational harm is done when one partner thinks of themselves more highly than the other or feels more deserving than the other. Perhaps you have heard someone say, "I bring home the paycheck around here so it's mine to decide how to use." This thoughtless and selfish attitude diminishes the worth of the other partner and is destructive to the marital community. It is equally destructive where one partner is lazy and slothful, "freeloading " on the other. While the income earned is likely to be different between partners, there should be a balance in the overall contribution that they are making to the relationship and toward the goals that they have established.

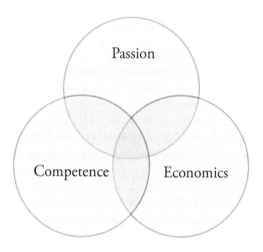

Since work is such an important part of life and occupies a huge portion of our time, ideally our work is in the intersection of passion, competence, and economics. What are you passionate about? What is it that you are or can become really good at? Is there a demand for this skill in the marketplace? If you are preparing for work, look for an opportunity in which you can answer yes to all three questions. If you are already working, assess your current job and see if you are in the sweet spot where passion, competence, and economics intersect. If you are not in the sweet spot, then where are you? If you are passionate about an area and the economics are there for a meaningful return for your work effort, then what can you do to gain the competence to be employable? (Example: I love helping people deal with life challenges and, if I were a licensed mental health therapist, I could earn a living doing this. To accomplish this will require that I get a master's degree in an appropriate field and pass a state licensing exam).

What if you are passionate about an activity and can become really good at it, but there is limited demand in the marketplace for such skills? Individuals with a passion for sports, for animals, for music, for entertainment, or art for instance may find themselves in this situation. In these venues there are a few individuals who truly do make it so that the economics do work in a big way for them, but for most individuals, the path to success is rocky and may lead to a financial dead end. This is a difficult situation to be in and there are no straightforward answers. For some pursuing their passion above all things is of the upmost importance even if it means living at lower standard. Others may be able to find something to do with their passion and competence that somehow connects to the economics of life. For instance, if you love sports (or music or art or___) but it is unlikely that you will be able to make it as a paid professional in this area, is there a way that you can combine it with another skill set like being an educator in order to make the economics work?

What if you have competence in an area where there is a demand for your services so that the economics work but you lack passion for what you are doing? This is the situation for many people. While it may not be the optimal situation, it does provide the financial base which allows for an individual to engage in the activities they are passionate about during their non-work time. Many choose to use their discretionary time to pursue activities that they enjoy or are in service to others, but are not financially remunerative.

GENEROSITY

Just as parents delight in providing for their children, God delights in providing for us. He wants to provide for us to meet our needs and for us to be a witness to the world of the joy that results from following him. As we are faithful in using the resources God has entrusted to us, he is able to entrust us with more. If we are open only to receiving from God and not to blessing others with what we have been given, we run the risk of becoming a salty, dead sea with only an inlet rather than a beautiful, freshwater lake that has both an inlet and an outlet. Thinking about God's work and the needs of others as a financial management priority helps us remember that we are stewards of what God has entrusted to us.

Luke quotes Jesus as saying, "Give, and it will be given to you. A good measure, pressed down, shaken together and running over will be poured into your lap. For with the measure you use, it will be measured to you" (Luke 6:38). God asks us to give off the top and not what's left over at the bottom: "Honor the Lord with your wealth, with the first fruits of all your crops; then your barns will be filled to overflowing, and your vats will brim over with new wine"(Prov. 3:9–10).

We see several types of giving described in the Bible. One is giving as praise to God. This is beautifully portrayed in the Old Testament, where people gave a freewill offering for the building of the Tabernacle (Exod. 25:1–2) and in the New Testament where a woman anointed Jesus with a very expensive perfume (Matt. 26:6–13).

Tithing (giving ten percent of income to God) is a principal that predates the law of Moses (see Gen. 14:17–20 and 38:20–22) and is an area where God himself invites us to fully trust in his provision (Mal. 3:8–10).

In the New Testament, Jesus acknowledges the religious leaders for giving a tithe, but admonishes them for not keeping more important aspects of the law such as justice, mercy, and faithfulness. He told them they should be doing both things (Matt. 23:23).

Another area in which we are instructed to give is to help other Christians who are in need (Rom. 12:13). The goal is to recognize that as Christians we are in a community to mutually support each other.

In addition to helping Christians in need, Scripture is clear that helping the poor is another giving priority In talking about the future kingdom of heaven, Jesus makes it clear that what we do for the poor we are doing to him. In Matthew 25, he says, "I was hungry and you gave me something to eat … whatever you did for one of the least of these … you did for me."

As believers in Christ, we are called to give for the purpose of investing in the gospel and supporting full-time Christian workers. In writing to the Corinthian church Paul asks: "Don't you know that those who work in the temple get their food from the temple, and those who serve at the altar share in what is offered on the altar? In the same way, the Lord has commanded that those who preach the gospel should receive their living from the gospel" (I Cor. 9:13–14).

Giving helps us become outward focused, and it furthers God's purposes on earth. We can give as a praise to God, to support fellow believers in need, to help the poor, and to invest in the spread of the gospel by supporting Christian workers. When a person gives what they do not own (because it belongs to God already) they are really transferring stewardship responsibility to another party.

In marriage, it is important that both partners are able to think through important questions related to giving, to discuss these questions openly and honestly as they each present their ideas, and work to reach agreement with each other on household giving levels and priorities.[1] Here are some questions to consider:

- What do you think about the idea of taking a portion of what we earn as a family off the top and giving it away? What amount or percent of income should we target to give?
- If we tithe at ten percent of income, how much is that in dollars per year? How does that compare with our recent giving?
- If we are having trouble making ends meet now, what adjustments can we make to allow us to increase our giving?
- What long term giving stretch goal can we establish (something that may seem impossible given our present circumstances)?
- How can we give time, skills, and other resources as part of our generosity?

Once you as a couple have established a plan for giving, then the next step is to prayerfully consider where the funds should go. Giving can include church, Christian ministries, and other passion areas (such as homelessness, human trafficking, arts, education, etc.).

If you are part of a local church and that church is sharing the gospel and equipping and encouraging you in your faith, then you will want to direct a significant portion of your giving there. Giving at your church may include supporting the general budget, as well as missions or special projects.

Now look beyond your church to other nonprofit organizations that may be in your community or around the world. These organizations likely have a specific focus such as: global evangelism, Christian education, hunger relief, help for the homeless, Bible distribution, promotion of biblical gender equality, prison ministry, Bible translation, disaster relief, clean water, medical ministry, housing for the poor, child sponsorship, drug rehabilitation, helping victims of sexual trafficking or of domestic abuse, among many others. The focus of these ministries offers an opportunity for us as believers to reach deeper into our communities and around the nation and world with a focused objective in mind.

Consider support for ministries that overlap with your interests and passions.

- What ministries outside our church ignite our interest?
- Does the ministry support biblical reasons to give?
- Is the ministry using their funds wisely?[2]
- What commitment of finances and/or time do we want to give to the organizations we have selected?

As you discuss giving together as a couple, it is likely that there will be some areas in which you are both enthused about supporting and other areas in which one of you has the most interest. One way to decide how to allocate your giving is to have each person list the amount of support that they would like to give to each organization with the total equaling your giving budget. Compare your answers and discuss them with each other, working to arrive at a figure that honors and respects the views of each individual. In some cases, when one partner learns how significant a particular giving area is to the other partner and why, they will want to increase their allocation to this area. In other instances, the solution may be to average the amounts each has listed separately.

If you want to give regularly to support your church and a number of other nonprofits, you may want to minimize the "chore" function of the giving, which can end up taking a lot of time. One way of eliminating the hassle of writing a check is to set up an automatic debit from your bank account on a monthly basis for the amount that you wish to give. (If you do a substantial amount of giving to many places, you might want to consider an organization that does the work for you.) If you do set up automatic giving, take time to periodically review where the funds are going to see if they match your current giving priorities. If you want to give by individual check to the organization, you can reduce the time factor by writing checks less often and for a larger dollar amount. If you are doing the giving on your own, you might want to have a separate savings account that you can put funds into, so that when special needs arise that you want to support, you will have the funds already set aside to give.

WISE SPENDING

It seems like wherever we go and whatever we do, we are bombarded with ads for goods and services. Madison Avenue works hard to convince us we need the products they are selling. They have an artful way of taking a product as basic as toothpaste and equating with it sex appeal. For most of us, it's much easier to spend money than to earn it. When budgets are limited and two people in a relationship have different opinions about spending, setting up rules of the road for spending is critical. Without that, your relationship is ripe for disagreements over spending. It is particularly hurtful when one party spends money on something for his or her gratification without getting buy-in from the other party. When two people work together and seek agreement on spending priorities they can help to counteract the natural impulse to over spend.

A budget is a plan to ensure that the money that you earn goes for the priorities that you have established. Both partners need to be involved in the creation of the household budget. Start with the sources of income you have and subtract funds you have prioritized for giving and those that are needed to pay taxes. The remaining amount is available to support current living expenses, to have a debt and buffer fund to handle past debts and larger less frequent outlays, and for longer term saving and investing.

Living expenses can be divided into fixed (i.e. monthly mortgage payment, insurance) and variable (gas, food, clothing). Track what you are spending in each area. If you find it difficult to make ends meet, then you will want to sharpen your pencil to look for opportunities to stretch your budget. This could involve making a lifestyle change to reduce or eliminate a fixed expenditure (like a change in housing or vehicle ownership) or it could mean giving greater attention to variable expenses.[3]

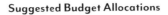

Suggested Budget Allocations

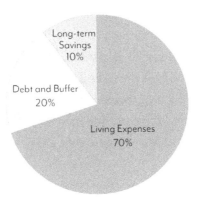

Long-term Savings 10%

Debt and Buffer 20%

Living Expenses 70%

For larger purchases, take time to prayerfully consider the expense as a couple and evaluate it. If you aren't in agreement, wait. The following are some questions to ask about the proposed purchase:

- Does it promote family unity? Are both parties in the relationship in agreement?
- Is it providing a positive contribution to family time, spiritual growth, or another family value?
- Is its value increasing or decreasing?
- Is the price right?
    - Is this the best time to buy?
    - If it is a sale, is it a current model?
    - If it is a sale, are you actually saving money or is it a marketing ploy?
- Can another item be substituted?
- Are there ongoing expenses we need to budget for?
- Can we afford the item and do we really need it?

The more significant the purchase, the greater the time that should be spent in answering the above questions. While one party in the relationship may take the lead in researching the answer to a question or questions, it is important that the information gained be presented truthfully to the other party and that both reach agreement before a purchase decision is made. As a general principle, the more significant the purchase the more important that agreement be reached.

To give each partner in the relationship some individual financial freedom, include some amount of "mad money" in your monthly budget. This is money for each individual to spend for miscellaneous small purchases as they choose—whether for a pedicure, a ticket to a sporting event, or a specialty espresso drink. The key is to agree to the dollar amount and have this amount included in the budget.

What about borrowing and buying on credit? The widespread availability of consumer credit has made it possible for households to make purchases now and pay for them later. Finance charges can result in a severe strain on family finances and a significant emotional burden for the relationship. When a couple is deeply in debt it is hard for them to be joyful about God's provision and difficult to be generous in their giving. The apostle Paul encourages believers to "Let no debt remain outstanding except the continuing debt to love one another" (Rom. 13:8). Proverbs warns us that "The rich rule over the poor, and the borrower is servant to the lender" (Prov. 22:7). Debt can create a situation of bondage rather than the freedom that God would have for us as his children. For a couple contemplating a purchase that would be financed with credit, talk through the previous questions on a large purchase, then ask the following questions:

- Is this essential for our work (example - a computer)?
- Can we buy the item used and not go into debt (for example, a used vehicle)?
- Have we prayed about the purchase, examined our motivations, and sought godly counsel?
- How we will adjust our future budget to pay for the debt being incurred in as short a time as possible?
- How does buying compare with renting over time (such as for a home)?
- Are we both in agreement about the planned course of action?

The debt and buffer fund described in the suggested budget above is designed to accumulate funds to make larger, less frequent purchases such as a large appliance or motor vehicle, or to make payments on existing debt. If you have no debt (other than your home mortgage expense), then use the funds that accumulate in this fund to make those purchases. If you have existing debt, then use this fund to pay off this debt as quickly as you can.

Paying off debt takes a disciplined strategy. While making at least the minimum payment required on each loan, apply your largest payment to the loan which has the highest rate of interest. Once this has been paid off (the loan with the highest interest rate), take the money that you were paying on it, and add it tothe payment you are making to the loan with the next highest rate of interest, etc. until all loans have been paid off.

Some couples who have been careful about their own finances have gotten trapped into the situation of cosigning on a loan for a friend or family member. Lenders love cosigners because it provides the lender with additional collateral. The book of Proverbs has numerous warnings about the dangers of cosigning (see Prov. 6:1–5). If you want to help a friend or family member, then go ahead and give them what you can afford but avoid cosigning. It can be costly to you and destructive to the friendships of those involved.

Dealing with Unexpected Loss

Following Jesus does not give us an umbrella that makes us immune from the storms of life. Car accidents, medical issues, fire, theft, loss of a job, death of a partner, and natural disasters can create severe financial storms. When we face such situations we might ask, "Where is God? Why has he let this happen to me?" During times like these, we need to remember that God is with us and his love for us is never-failing. The prophet Habakkuk stated it well when he said:

> Though the fig tree does not bud and there are no grapes on the vines, though the olive crop fails and the fields produce no food, though there are no sheep in the pen and no cattle in the stalls, yet I will rejoice

in the Lord, I will be joyful in God my Savior. The Sovereign Lord is my strength; he makes my feet like the feet of a deer, he enables me to go on the heights (Hab. 3:17–19).

For a couple, the burden of an unexpected loss can create a severe relational and financial strain. The "blame game" can ultimately tear a couple apart. Alternatively, the couple can draw closer as they express their fears, worries, and doubts with each other, and as they seek God's guidance and provision through the difficult time they are facing. Although a loss may be unexpected, there are ways to prepare for potential losses.

Consider as an example the risk of a house fire. Things that could be done before a fire include taking safety steps to reduce the risk of fire, installing smoke alarms to warn of a fire, having a fire drill in the event an evacuation is needed, and insuring the home against loss should a fire occur.

Another example to consider: One member of the household unexpectedly loses their job. Discuss with each other ways that the potential losses could be mitigated through financial management:

- What role should a long-term savings program play?
- What role should insurance play?
- In what areas are there government programs that would help financially for an unexpected loss

(unemployment insurance, flood insurance, worker's compensation, for example)?

- How can benevolence in the body of Christ help mitigate the burden of unexpected loss?

SAVING, INVESTING, AND PLANNING FOR THE FUTURE

God frequently provides for our needs before the need occurs. Saving provides a way for us to set aside a portion of our current earnings to meet our future needs. We see this in the cycle of the seasons, where food produced in summer can be harvested and used in winter. We see this in the cycle of life, too. We start out as a tiny infant relying on the provision of our parents, grow into adulthood and take our place in the workplace, and then move into eventual physical decline.

One of the key reasons for saving is to be able to provide for our needs during retirement so as to not be a burden on others: "After all, children should not have to save up for their parents, but parents for their children" (2 Cor. 12: 14). We are instructed that our family should be a priority in our plans: "If anyone does not provide for his relatives, and especially for his immediate family, he has denied the faith and is worse than an unbeliever" (I Tim. 5: 8). If you have children, longer term savings can help them with college or vocational education.

Other reasons for longer term saving include accumulating funds for investment in a home or business and providing for unexpected losses or disruptions in income that will occur. As you consider a longer term savings program reflect on these questions as a couple:

- What longer terms needs should we be saving for?
- What amount or percent of our income that we can set aside longer term savings?
- Is the amount we can set aside going to be adequate to meet our future needs?
- If not, what can we do to increase our long term savings over time? Ideas here might include devoting more toward savings as debts are retired, working more, or setting aside a pay increase to increase the amount saved.

Longer term savings need to be invested to maximize their value over time. We see an example of investing in Proverbs with the woman who "considers a field and buys it; out of her earnings she plants a vineyard" (Prov. 31:16). In the parable of the talents Jesus shares the story of servants who were given various talents to manage for their owner. When the owner returned and demanded an account of the managers' performance, the ones who had been given more and invested what they had been given wisely were entrusted with more, but the one who had been given little buried it in the ground and gave it back to the owner. The owner harshly rebuked the one who just returned what he had been given saying that at a minimum the funds should have been deposited to earn interest (Matt: 25:14–30).

There are a myriad of investment options and opportunities and investing takes time and attention. Usually there is a relation between risk and reward—the greater the potential reward, the greater the risk. Investments that are illiquid (not easy to convert to cash like real estate) may return more over time but do so at additional risk. Leverage (using some borrowed funds) increases risk and the potential for loss or gain. There is value in diversification. Things that look too good to be true probably are. Professional management fees and transactions fees can significantly reduce returns over time. Don't get into an investment you don't understand and aren't comfortable with. Once you have made an investment, pay attention and monitor it. Even if one of you is going to manage your investments, take time to discuss and understand investments together as a couple.

As you consider various investment strategies, here are some questions to discuss as a couple:

- What is the level of risk that we are comfortable with?
- What types of investments fit our desired risk profile?
- Do we understand clearly the nature of each investment we are considering?
- How can we diversify our investments to reduce risk?
- Do we both agree on the investment strategy?
- Do we have a will to specify how our estate should be divided up when we are gone and (if minor children are in the home) who we want to care for our children?

There is definitely a balance we should strike in our savings and investing as we set aside funds for anticipated future needs but avoid storing up wealth for wealth's sake alone. Jesus tells the parable of the rich fool who ran out of room to store all his crops and decided to tear down his barns so he could build even bigger barns. His greedy intent was to store up things for himself rather than being rich toward God and the result was that his life ended abruptly. Jesus warns us to be on guard against all kinds of greed, noting that a person's life does not consist in the abundance of possessions (Luke 12:13–21).

Numerous passages in the Bible promote good financial management and planning for the future, but we are to balance our own efforts with the realization that God is our ultimate provider and that we need not worry:

> So do not worry, saying, 'What shall we eat?' or 'What shall we drink?' or 'What shall we wear?' For the pagans run after all these things, and your heavenly Father knows that you need them. But seek first his kingdom and his righteousness, and all these things will be given to you as well. Therefore, do not worry about tomorrow, for tomorrow will worry about itself. Each day has enough trouble of its own (Matt. 6: 31–34).

Summary

Financial management can be a great source of strength for a Christian couple. When we recognize that we are stewards of God's creation, then this mutually shared attitude creates the foundation for decisions affecting work, giving, spending, and saving. While each person in the relation brings different abilities and strengths, major financial priorities need to be jointly established by mutual consent in an environment of openness and honesty. Doing this with love and respect for each other, honors each person and allows for them and the marriage relationship to flourish.

– 5 –

Forgiveness, Apology, and Reconciliation

Lynne Nelson

Forgiving does not erase the bitter past. A healed memory is not a deleted memory. Instead, forgiving what we cannot forget creates a new way to remember. We change the memory of our past into a hope for our future.
—Lewis B. Smedes' The Art of Forgiving[1]

As a human, you can fully expect to be hurt and wounded by others. You can also expect that other people will experience sadness and emotional pain due to your behavior. These behaviors may or may not be intentional, but either way, how do you live through and beyond this kind of pain? If deeply serious pain comes from your life partner, how do you go on? Is it even possible for you to reconcile and deeply enjoy life together again? This chapter will explore concepts of forgiveness, apology, and reconciliation—actions that take courage and strength, yet promise renewed freedom and peace.

What kinds of situations need forgiving? Some problems may just be inconveniences that can be overlooked. In relationship, couples have disagreements or fights; learning to understand and validate each other and ourselves is an amazingly helpful process. Beyond commonplace arguments, most of us will also be faced with life-changing offenses in which we feel deeply wronged. All of these levels of pain call for an attitude of grace as we plunge into healing and/or forgiveness processes. The discussions in this chapter are focused on making a wise and careful response to some of the bigger grievances you face in life.

COMMON QUESTIONS ABOUT FORGIVENESS

IS IT BETTER TO IGNORE THE INJURY?

You might wonder if you should ignore an offense done to you. It is up to each person to ponder and determine if small, bothersome acts are really issues or not. For example, when your spouse frowns at you, are they trying to insult you, or, are they perhaps trying to answer a problem rolling around in their mind? This may be a situation where you overlook a small, unintentional offense, or you may feel you need to discuss your feelings with your partner.

Forgiveness is not about denial, pretending something didn't happen, or saying a real issue was no big deal. Emotionally healthy people acknowledge and feel their true emotions. Forgiveness is also not about excusing behaviors. Saying "They couldn't help it," or "They were raised that way, it's not their fault!" is not properly dealing with the issue.

Should People Forgive and Forget? ✕

Forgiveness is not about forgetting. We are human, and we remember. If you say, "I'll just forget about it," you are just fooling yourself. You might be able to speak and act and smile like you forgot, but your body remembers, and your emotional pain may even come out in the form of physical ailments. Neither does forgiveness erase a wrong; it does not turn the wrong into something right. Lewis Smedes writes,

> When we forgive evil we do not excuse it, we do not tolerate it, we do not smother it. We look the evil full in the face, call it what it is, let its horror shock and stun and enrage us, and only then do we forgive it.[2]

Why Is It So Hard to Forgive?

A person's state of unforgiveness may be a form of self-protection. Maybe you don't want to face your pain directly because you believe you had some role in the situation. Or, perhaps, you think that if you forgive, it means it wasn't so important or you weren't actually violated. But the truth is that it does matter, and your inner self and your body still feel the pain of the offense done to you. You need to deal with offensive situations and actions.[3]

What are the Benefits of Forgiveness?

It is likely that the offense you seek to forgive has changed your life in a significantly negative way. You have recognized your pain and your loss; you are in the ensuing struggle to follow God's design for forgiveness. However, as you walk through the forgiveness process you may find a new sense of freedom, new passions, and new ability in your life. You may experience some of the following:

- You have learned from the experience and are stronger for it.
- You have a broader perspective of pain in the world, and increased compassion.
- You are no longer obsessed with the wrong done.
- Your creativity flows more freely.
- You find a new purpose and a way to help or advocate for others.

The process of forgiving is not only about the other person. It is also about you. Whether or not reconciliation occurs, Robert Enright says:

> Forgiveness actually can alter your sense of identity, your sense of who you are. You are no longer a victim of others or of your past. You are no longer defined by certain events that may have occurred years ago. As you change how you think, feel, and behave, your very sense of yourself may change for the better.[4]

Forgiveness releases us from the depth of pain imposed on us by another. As Lewis Smedes wrote, "Our history is an inevitable component of our being. One thing only can release us from the grip of our history. That one thing is forgiveness."[5]

SIGNIFICANT ISSUES DISRUPTING MARRIAGES

Three areas deeply disrupt or destroy the strong marriage bond: attachment wounds, domestic abuse, and affairs. Professional intervention is recommended to help couples work through these significant issues and ideally move toward apology, forgiveness, behavior change, and—when it is deemed to be safe as well as desirable—reconciliation.

1. *Attachment Injuries.* Couples need a secure attachment; a trust that when either one is hurting or in need, the other will be responsive and available to them.[6] An injury happens when one spouse is in extreme need and the other seems to dismiss or ignore that need instead of responding and engaging. For example, a husband feels unable to help his wife when she is in childbirth, so he goes for a round of golf. Or, when news of a family death comes and one partner disengages by leaving the home rather than processing together. Another attachment injury could occur if one person is physically or emotionally exhausted and in dire need of help or a reassuring presence, yet their partner leaves to keep a social coffee time with friends. Couples need to address and heal these wounds through a process of understanding, making apologies, forgiving, and, hopefully, reconciling.

2. *Domestic Abuse.* Within marriages, domestic abuse is more prevalent than commonly thought. It is estimated that

twenty-five to fifty percent of couples experience physical and/or psychological abuse.[7] It is traumatic to find that the vows you as husband and wife made to each other, to love and care for each other, are being broken by abuse. Abuse causes emotional distance, intensive conflict, and loss of trust between partners. Domestic abuse is a problem within the church as well as in secular households.[8]

Domestic violence is an area so shaming that the victims often remain quiet and the perpetrators keep their horrible secrets. Intervention is essential: victims need to be empowered and upheld by their friends, their communities, and their churches, and abusers need to be brought to accountability. Sadly, abuse perpetrators do not usually change their behavior, but victims can free themselves through forgiveness.

3. *Affairs.* The injunction against adultery is a foundation of the marriage covenant in the Judeo-Christian tradition (see Deut. 5:18). Yet research within Western culture reveals that fifty percent of marriages—in the church, as well as the broader society—experience either sexual or emotional affairs by one or both spouses.[9] In the West, while monogamy is purported to be esteemed, it is also undermined by sexualizing messages and images. Serious wounding occurs as a result of marital infidelity. The tenets of forgiveness are very pertinent for the healing of the persons wounded by affairs. According to researcher Shirley Glass, "It's possible to reach a functional level of *recovery* without forgiveness, but it's not possible to

achieve final *healing* of yourself or your relationship without forgiveness."[10] This forgiveness may need to be *one-way* from the wounded person if the straying partner fails to be repentant and make change. Or, both marriage partners may come on board to journey through the long process of apology, forgiveness, and then, possibly, reconciliation.

THE PROCESS OF FORGIVENESS

Forgiving is a long and arduous process. It may begin with a decision, yet the process of forgiving is more like a journey. The offended person needs support, care, and healing over a period of time. Sadly, churches may push people to forgive quickly rather than work through the process.[11] Mary's story illustrates this issue:

> When my pastors and church friends found out that Edward and I were separated, and even though they knew it was because of his violence, one of the very first reactions from everybody in the church was, "Well, you need to forgive him," Their response was devastating to me. It was as if what they know about my husband's abuse didn't matter. "Forgive and forget," they all said. I couldn't do either at the time, so I felt like such a sinner.[12]

While surveying pastor's positions on forgiveness and reconciliation in abusive marriages, A. Miles spoke with one prominent pastor who had learned of a husband who abused his wife.[13] The pastor confirmed that the abuse was wrong, but then he encouraged the victim to forgive as soon as possible.

Respect the process of forgiveness.

Forgiveness was not respected as a process, and neither the offense nor the need for behavior change was addressed.

Experts and researchers in the field of forgiveness and trauma don't encourage quick forgiveness. Instead, they explain processes which you walk through over time as you work toward forgiveness and continue the journey of your life.[14] There is usually a correlation between the depth of the hurt and the amount of time it takes to move into forgiveness. It requires searching one's heart, pondering, and praying. Don't rush yourself or others into an attempted quick-fix statement of "I forgive you." Another area that takes time is the process of grieving over the loss that you have suffered. Forgiveness is an emotional letting go. It is important to recognize your loss, to acknowledge your loss, and consider how your life would have been different had you not incurred this loss. You will then better understand exactly what you are forgiving.

Often, when you resolve to forgive, you may not feel any different at first. As time goes on and you keep reminding yourself that you have chosen to forgive, your emotions are likely to be lighter and more relaxed regarding the incident. As you develop compassion and empathy for the offender, you may even be able to wish well for that person.

Forgiveness and acceptance are not the same. When you accept a person, it does not imply that you have forgiven that person. "We accept people for who they *are*, we forgive them for the bad they *did*."[15] In the context of a marriage relationship, you will aspire to both accept and forgive the offending person in order to keep the relationship.

It may be harder to forgive when the offender does not acknowledge any wrong, or is naive about the pain his or her behavior has caused. Yes, it would be easier to forgive if they were repentant, but that may not happen. You can then choose to freely grant forgiveness regardless of the offender's stance. This is called *one-way* forgiveness. In this case you realize that forgiveness comes from inside you and is not dependent on the state of the offender. In a way, not forgiving because the offender has not repented leaves the victimized person attached to the offender. As you focus on her or him with anger, hate, frenzy, or dismay, your efforts are spent hanging on to your anguish, rather than stepping into new freedom and gaining happiness.

Consider the story of the prodigal son in Luke 15. He did more than take money from his father and use it in a reprehensible way. He insulted the very core of his father's being. Yet, "while he was still a long way off, his father saw him coming. Filled with love and compassion, the father ran to his son, embraced him, and kissed him" (Luke 15:20b, NLT). When they embraced, the father did not know if his son was repentant. This father intended his forgiveness to flow to his son even before he knew anything about his son's heart attitude.

By granting one-way forgiveness, you will have changed the offender's impact on you, but you will not have changed the offender. Since your forgiveness does not mean that the offender has changed, it does not automatically make that relationship safe again.

The REACH Model

Forgiveness is an internal process. It happens when the offended person chooses to release the offender. Everett Worthington has designed a practical approach that he calls the REACH model of forgiveness.[16] As you work through each letter, you build onto your forgiveness process in a step by step manner.

R = Recall. Recall the wrong that was done to you. Be honest with yourself about the pain; don't soften or minimize the actual impact of that pain. You need to know and feel what you are forgiving. To do this you must be specific, "Remember, you cannot forgive in the abstract. Forgiveness occurs when you work through *specific events with specific people*."[17]

E = Empathy. Strive to develop some level of empathy toward the one who hurt you. Imagine what life events may have put the offender into the place where she or he might do the harm that impacts you so severely. Remember that empathy may not come until later, when further healing has occurred.

A = Altruistic. Grant forgiveness as an altruistic gift. A part of this process is deciding that the offender will owe you nothing. You are giving the gift of forgiveness freely and without demand. You do not try to get even.

C = Commit. You commit to forgive in some public or community setting, or with one other person. Your choice to forgive will be made more solid as you speak of it to another.

H = Hold. Once you forgive, you need to hold onto the decision. You will need to remind yourself at future times that you have in fact forgiven that person of his or her offense.

Corrie ten Boom brings us an example of forgiveness. She was a Christian arrested for hiding Jews during World War II, and had been taken to Ravensbruck concentration camp where she was degraded and humiliated by Nazi guards. In 1947 Corrie was publicly speaking the message of God's forgiveness. After speaking, she recognized a former Nazi guard coming toward her. He announced that he had become a Christian and knew that God forgave him for his cruel behaviors—now he was asking for Corrie's forgiveness. She reported that she felt frozen as she recalled the scene of the delousing shower in the camp where he had been a guard. As she prayed for Jesus' help, she had the ability to lift her hand and take the outstretched hand of the former guard. As she did so,

> The current started in my shoulder, raced down my arm, sprang into our joined hands. And then this healing warmth seemed to flood my whole being, bringing tears to my eyes. 'I forgive you, brother! ...With all my heart!'[18]

The guard no longer had power over Corrie when she granted forgiveness. She concluded saying "I had never known God's love so intensely as I did then."[19]

Beyond One-Way Forgiveness

Apology

Apology is an action on the part of the offender. It is good if the offender proactively comes forward and apologizes. This takes a humble state and much courage; you do this out of respect for God, and for the person you have hurt. In marriage, your apology and request for forgiveness can help move the two of you toward oneness again.

The Bible speaks of two kinds of sorrow: "For the kind of sorrow God wants us to experience leads us away from sin and results in salvation. There's no regret for that kind of sorrow. But worldly sorrow, which lacks repentance, results in spiritual death" (2 Cor. 7:10, NLT).

Godly sorrow, then, involves a repentant attitude. That is, making change within your inner self as well as in your outer behavior. Webster's Dictionary defines repent as: "To turn from sin and dedicate oneself to the amendment of one's life, to feel regret or contrition, or to change one's mind."[20] The feeling of repentance has to do with an inner attitude causing one to want to make a positive change in behavior.

Worldly sorrow is when you are sorry basically because your

action has made your life inconvenient. An example of worldly sorrow is saying "I said I am sorry, didn't I?" or even, "I am sorry you feel that way." This is defensive and does not take responsibility for any wrong on your part. It is rather like telling the injured person to be quiet and pretend the offense never occurred. This is not a means to peace or reconciliation. To make a sincere and effective apology, the offender needs to acknowledge, understand, and validate the deep pain inflicted on the wounded person; they need to feel remorse and sorrow for their actions. Finally, they need to join with their spouse in creating a healing plan and committing to renewed plans for their future. Below, author Sue Johnson relays an example of a meaningful apology from Ted to his wife, Vera:

> I really let you down, didn't I? I wasn't there for you. I am so sorry, Vera. I got all overwhelmed and left you to stare down your enemy by yourself. It's hard for me to admit this. I don't want to see myself as the kind of person, the kind of husband who would let you down like this. But I did it. You had a right to get angry. I never saw my support as that important. But I know now that I hurt you very badly. I wasn't sure what to do, so I dithered and did nothing. I want to try to make this better. If you will let me.[21]

There are several critical elements in Ted's apology. Ted cares about the pain that Vera suffered when he ignored her. He then tells her that he sees her hurt and assures her that he views her pain as legitimate. He takes responsibility for his role in creating her pain and specifically states what he did wrong. Ted explains his disappointment in himself and commits to being present with his wife to help her heal and to rebuild a different future.

Reconciliation

Is forgiveness the same as reconciliation? Does forgiveness mean you are bound to reconcile? When you forgive an offense, is your trust automatically restored with the offending person? Do you no longer need to address the hurtful issue? Is it all behind you now? The answers to all these questions are "no."

Forgiveness and reconciliation are not one and the same. Forgiveness is an internal process within the heart of one person; reconciliation is interpersonal, that is, between two or more people. True reconciliation is not one-sided. Lewis B. Smedes wrote, "It takes one person to forgive, it takes two people to be reunited."[22] When the offending person understands the pain they have inflicted, makes an apology, takes responsibility, and shows empathy for the offended, then the two parties can begin exploring what is needed to reunite and reconcile the relationship.

Before reentering a relationship quickly with a person who has deeply offended you, it is wise to see a change in that person's behavior. Recall that in the story of Joseph (Genesis 42–45), he did not immediately trust his brothers when they arrived in Egypt. Joseph tested them. He overheard his brothers lamenting that they had sold Joseph into slavery. Then Joseph's brother Judah insisted on taking the position of being a slave himself in the place of his youngest brother, Benjamin, for the sake of their father, Jacob. Joseph's heart seemed to soften as he wept and then told his brothers the truth of who he was; he embraced Benjamin and kissed his brothers. Joseph offered his entire family a safe home during the time of famine. Joseph was able to renew their relationship after he could see that they had a godly fear, and probably remorse, over their former bad behavior.

Serious offenses destroy trust, and in marriage, trust is essential for unity, passion, joy, and confidence in the relationship. If and when both parties desire, the process of reconciliation can move forward. But first, there needs to be an apology in which the injuring party takes responsibility for their actions, and a discussion in which both persons speak, listen, and seek to understand the other.

Now comes the time to rework and reestablish the plans and expectations between the two of you for your renewed relationship. The patterns and steps you walk through in your forgiveness-to-reconciliation journey are a courageous pathway. This process invariably takes much listening, talking, and understanding. The journey for you as a couple is precious; it can recreate connection, passion, and vitality within your relationship.

RESTITUTION

"Bah, humbug!" Ebenezer Scrooge, Charles Dickens' famous character, hated Christmas traditions and generosity. Instead, he was mean and miserly. After visits from the ghosts of

Christmas past, present, and future, Scrooge had a change of heart *and* behavior. He became generous and kind, sociable and light-hearted. He gave magnanimously to the poor and to his employee in need of a raise. Scrooge was making restitution for his past.

Zacchaeus also made restitution. He was a wealthy and unscrupulous tax collector, but when Jesus confronted him, Zacchaeus had a change of heart and promised to make up for his past cheating.

> But Zacchaeus stood up and said to the Lord, "Look, Lord! Here and now I give half of my possessions to the poor, and if I have cheated anybody out of anything, I will pay back four times the amount." Jesus approved, saying to him, "Today salvation has come to this house." (Luke 19:9)

Repentance may spur a person to attempt some restitution. Making restitution involves action for the benefit of the one you have offended. Restitution must be offered to the injured person with empathy and in an honest, caring spirit. The steps of restitution need to be acts genuinely offered for the purpose of aiding in the recovery of, or otherwise helping, the injured one. These acts cannot just be a peace offering given in an attempt to make the offender feel better.

Yet some injustices are too big or too deep to compensate for or to adequately repair; that is why we must see that when the injured person offers forgiveness, it is an altruistic gift to the offender. We need to grieve these losses that can never be fully replaced. The loss has changed your life in some significant way and may involve pain occurring over many years.

Making steps of reparation or restitution shows that the offending person desires to be different and to live life in a new way. This can be beneficial to both parties. The offended person receives some help, and the offending person, who is remorseful and making restitution for the past, begins to gain a renewed sense of dignity.

God Has Forgiven Us and Asks Us to Forgive

God has given us the wonderful gift of forgiveness. In this great gift from God we experience his love and compassion for us. We each know the truth of our inner selves; we know that we need that forgiveness from God. Scripture tells us that "... if we confess our sins to him, he is faithful and just to forgive us our sin and to cleanse us from all wickedness (1 John 1:9, NLT). And his forgiveness is complete, removing our sin: "As far as the east is from the west" (Psalm 103:12).

Making the choice to follow God's direction to forgive urges us to go beyond our own pain in order to see the other person beyond their sin; all so that we can free ourselves from the entanglements of unforgiveness. Paul exhorts, "Be kind to one another, compassionate, forgiving one another just as God in Christ has forgiven you" (Eph. 4:31-32). In the Lord's Prayer, Jesus teaches us to ask our heavenly father to "Forgive us our sins, as we have forgiven those who sin against us" (Matt. 6:12, NLT).

Forgiveness does not erase wrongs or make them less than they are, but forgiveness can release us from the past, and open the way to possible reconciliation.

QUESTIONS FOR DISCUSSION AND REFLECTION

1. After reading this chapter, are there any false ideas about forgiveness that you have held? If not, what obstacles do you encounter when trying to forgive?
2. What part of the REACH model for forgiveness would you like to practice more?
3. What's the difference between one-way forgiveness and the processes of moving toward reconciliation?
4. What must happen first before reconciliation can take place?

– 6 –

Sacred Sexuality

Kelsey Siemens and Janelle Kwee

> "Sexuality is a beautiful, good, extremely powerful, sacred energy,
> given to us by God and experienced in every cell of our being as an
> irrepressible urge to overcome our incompleteness, to move toward
> unity and consummation with that which is beyond us."[1]
> —Ronald Rolheiser, The Holy Longing

The Genesis account of life before the fall speaks to what God intended for humanity. Here, we saw woman, man, and the divine living in perfect relationship—a space in which they mutually gave and received love, a space of intimacy, vulnerability, and complete nakedness. As the story goes, the fall created an urge to hide, to cover, and to live in shame. But there's good news: we do not have to live under this curse.

My (Kelsey) own story—my pain and transformation—motivated me to understand how we can move from living out our sexuality from a place of shame and silence to a place of communion and mutual love. Growing up in a religious community that, generally, only spoke about sexuality in terms of regulation of behavior ("shoulds and should nots"), I quickly internalized the idea that my sexuality was "dirty." The silence around my sexuality in my faith community was deafening. When I did hear about sexuality, it was typically framed from a place of fear.

When I was thirteen, my grandpa learned that I had "become a woman" at my first menses. He pulled me aside and began to weep. When I asked him what was wrong, he declared, "I don't want you to get pregnant like some of the other girls at my church." That summer, I was also told that my "kisses were like a rose" and that every time I kissed someone I would lose a petal. The individual who shared this suggested that my future husband would probably prefer not to receive "just a measly stem." These messages shaped the way I saw myself and my body.

As an adolescent, I felt shame as my body developed, as I experienced desire, and as I expressed my sexuality in ways that I felt were conflicting with the messages I heard. I felt excruciatingly alone in my shame. It was only when I got married that I felt like I had permission to explore my body, my sexuality, and my shame. The eventual spiritual shift in understanding that my body was just as valuable as my heart, mind, and spirit, allowed me to work toward embracing and affirming my sexuality.

This experience is not unique to me; Janelle and I have spent hours talking with Christian men and women about their sexual journeys. We wondered how other men and women—who were perhaps taught to believe that their sexuality is "of the flesh" or, in some way sinful—were able to then experience fulfilling, pleasurable, and connected sexual relationships? What were their journeys like? What lessons did they learn? How, if needed, did their healing take place? Our hope was that, by answering some of these questions, we would have insight into how to help men and women reclaim and express their sexuality with their whole selves.

Sexuality is the "physical, emotional, psychological, and spiritual energy that permeates, influences, and colors our entire being and personality in its quest for love, communion, friendship, wholeness, self-perpetuation, and self-transcendence."[2] This chapter is not intended to be a technical manual, but to encourage you to develop a positive and realistic view of sexuality as something that is worthy of attention in your marriage, and to encourage you to seek additional help and resources when you face sexual challenges. We hope that this chapter, drawing from our research,[3] speaks to you about the beautiful gift of sexuality. We invite you into a conversation about sex, and how your understanding has shaped your experiences. We explore the things that get in the way of experiencing our sexuality fully. We then highlight how we can journey toward healing. Finally, we outline ways to engage sexuality meaningfully in marriage. At the end of the chapter, we include exercises and discussion questions.

THREATS TO MUTUALITY AND EMBODIMENT IN RELIGIOUS (AND GENDERED) MESSAGING

While sexuality is a powerful and sacred gift, common messages about sexuality—including some of those communicated in Christian faith contexts—often get in the way of mutual intimacy and relational wholeness with one's partner and with God. In this section, we explore how these messages interfere with the potential for couples to experience mature and mutual love. In the section that follows, we offer a glimpse of how individuals and couples can choose paths of wholeness and healing in sexual embodiment.

THE PERFECT PICTURE: NAKED AND UNASHAMED

"The man and his wife were both naked and they felt no shame (Genesis 2:25)."

The story of sexuality begins with its perfect expression in the Garden of Eden, characterized by the experience of being *naked and unashamed*. The nakedness of Eden represents Adam and Eve's connection and harmony with God and creation, including their own physical bodies. In the creation story, Adam and Eve experience total freedom and vulnerability in their relationship with each other and with their Creator. With the fall, shame caused them to feel the need to hide and find clothing even as their Creator called out for them among the trees in the garden.

EMBODIMENT

The term *embodiment* describes the *experience* of one's body in the world.[4] Embodiment signifies awareness *as* a body rather than as self *with* a body. If this sounds new or even strange to you, it is likely because of dualistic ideas of the spirit or self as being separate from the body. Think, for a moment, about how you experience the world and express yourself through the senses of your body. Try to imagine being *you* in the body of someone else, perhaps of another gender or ethnic background or vastly different size. You'll probably appreciate that who you are is uniquely reflected in and shaped by your physical self. In *sexual* embodiment, one experiences his or her whole self through sexual intimacy, through and within one's body. Sexual embodiment is "in-touchness" with one's desire and physical state; in sexual expression, the whole self is connected in giving and receiving love.

SHAME

The legacy of the fall is apparent through societal and religious messages of subordination and dominance that reinforce sexual shame and prevent couples from enjoying full agency and connection.[5] It has been argued that "no other aspect of human activity has been as dysfunctionally shamed as much as our sexuality."[6] With the legacy of shame from the fall, marriage offers a space for the redemptive work of Christ to be expressed in mutual love.

Shame is, "an intensely painful [and universal] feeling or experience of believing we are flawed and therefore unworthy of acceptance or belonging."[7] Shame causes a person to see themselves through what they think others see rather than through their own experiences.[8] Complicating this is the fact that messages about sexuality are often contradictory and unattainable. For example, the socio-religious value for women to be pure and virginal is contrasted with dominant socio-cultural expectations for women to be seductive sexual objects.

Religious Messaging

Church and society communicate several messages about sexuality. Many people report that silence about sexuality was the norm at home or in the church. If sex was discussed, it was limited to a dualistic mentality: the body is separate from the spirit. Many of the messages also included oppressive gender scripts. Finally, men and women both report being bombarded with religious messages about "rules" of appropriate sexual behavior. We describe these messaging themes below.

"Sex is bad": Silence and Dualism

Not talking about sexuality openly or comfortably implies that sexuality ought to be kept hidden. Those who shared their stories described a culture of silence, such that the meaning of sexuality, sexual safety, and sexual relationships were rarely spoken about in their families and faith communities. Silence around something that is so essentially human adds to shame, leaving people with questions and discomfort, even when given the freedom to explore sexual expression openly in marriage. In a culture that sells sex as a commodity, silence is especially problematic.

In contrast to a whole view of the person, dualism divides an individual into opposite or separate parts. In the case of humans, the body is separated from the mind or spirit. This notion of separation lends itself to the idea that one part (spirit or mind) is "better" or opposed to the other (body or flesh). When the flesh or the body is conceived of as separate from the person rather than as the person, it seems less important. Inherent in many Christian messages about sexuality is an urging to "not give into the lusts of the flesh." One woman shared how she internalized this false binary: "I really thought my body was a sinful thing, with these desires and needs, and it was just ruining my spirituality. So it was this dichotomy, this dualism." Similarly, one man shared that his sense was that sex and sexuality were off limits, because if he experienced it, "God would be angry...that's sinful, and sinners go to hell."

Given the silence about sexuality in family and faith contexts, combined with a hyper-sexualized popular culture, it is not surprising that many people internalize the extreme message that sex is bad or *un*-spiritual. Reflecting a dualistic religious perspective that the spirit and body are juxtaposed as good and evil, one woman told us how her perspective was shaped: "My only awareness of sex was that it's dirty, and bad, and you shouldn't be thinking of those things."

Unfortunately, a negative view of the body and sex doesn't miraculously shift toward freedom with marriage. Sex-positive messages about the goodness, power, and creativity of the body need to be cultivated along with messages about safety, consent, responsibility, and decision-making. Messages about sexual safety and responsibility *and* the goodness and power of the body are both important so that women and men can lovingly encounter themselves and their partner.

Gendered Messages

Another form of dualism—that men are held in a higher place than women—is reflected in gendered messages about sexuality. Rachael Held Evans, author of *A Year of Biblical Womanhood*, writes about how Christian women are bombarded with conflicting messages about how they should live in their bodies. Popular culture tells women to dress in a way to *get* men to look at them, reinforcing that a woman's value is based on her sex appeal. Modesty culture, on the other extreme, suggests that women should dress a certain way to *prevent* men from looking at them. Both cultures are disempowering, placing "the impetus ... on the woman to accommodate her clothing or her body to the ... expectations of men."[9] In this light, modesty messages do not affirm self-love, dignity, and self-respect. They are a means by which women are supposed to prevent men from "lusting" after them.

As described above, modesty culture tells women how to dress in order to uphold the church's value of modesty. While the virtue of modesty in rejecting objectification has the potential to be empowering, the apparent rationale often given for women's responsibility for modesty is to protect themselves and men from "lusting" over their bodies. There iss an underlying theme that women are not only responsible for their own sexuality, but also for men's sexuality. One woman shared the perception of a friend who was dressing "immodestly,"sarcastically exclaiming, "Yeah, like she was being irresponsible because if boys lusted she would be the one held responsible for it, not them.... Yeah, because guys, *THEY CAN'T CONTROL THEMSELVES!*" This reflects a power imbalance in which women are in a position of needing to protect themselves from being sexually consumed or objectified, reflecting a deeply patriarchal culture. The presumption in this message, that men can't assume responsibility in their bodies, disempowers both men and women.

Have you ever found yourself believing that men *need* sex in a way that is not true for women? In reality, the dynamics of desire and arousal between partners are complex and cannot be reduced to gender. The narrative of *sex-is-for-men* is restricting, disempowering, and potentially shaming for both men and women. If the expectation is that men value and need sex as an intrinsic part of their masculinity, does it then undermine their masculinity to experience lower arousal? Similarly, with this belief, what does it mean for a woman to have—and express—sexual desires and needs? One woman spoke of how this message persistently impacted the way she experienced sexuality in her marriage, stating:

> I remember that even in our first year of marriage of being like, and even still sometimes, I get anxious about, ok "how is he doing, do we need to have sex soon because like, how are you doing, do you need to release some tension?" Not even thinking about myself in that [at] all.

In the view of sex-is-for-men where "dutiful" wives are guided by the mandate to never say "no" to their partner's needs, mutuality is lost and women's shame over their own sexuality is perpetuated. Privileging male sexuality impedes women's ability to explore sexuality without guilt or shame.[10] Sexuality becomes distorted by dominance and subordination, coming dangerously close to marital rape and abuse. Though sexuality at its best represents mutual intimacy, when either partner's right to fully consent is lost, their bodies are objectified.

RULES AND CONDEMNATION

With perhaps a noble aim to protect young people from being hurt, there seems to be an abundance of Christian guidelines about "should" and "should not" in terms of sexual expression. The rules seem to reinforce a sex-negative conversation where restriction of behavior is emphasized over embodied self-expression and responsibility. One woman shared a perception that "if you broke the rules [about sexuality] that means you can't be close to God." Black and white messaging does not promote critical thinking or sexual responsibility, but gives external measures for whether particular behaviors fit or don't fit the "rules" or accepted "code."

Related to this, there seems to be a harsher standard of judgment pertaining to sins of a sexual nature. Complicating this, many Christian communities have codes of conduct by which members are expected to abide, and sexual transgressions appear to be more "measurable" than sins of the heart. Recalling the judgment unique to "sexual sins," one woman told about her experience at a private Christian school,

> There is not a lot of grace when you mess up. Like, if you were to say get pregnant, you couldn't continue going there [to the school]. Or if you decided that maybe you thought you were bisexual, you couldn't keep going there. And I just don't think that that's like Jesus.

This increases fear and shame resulting in people feeling alienated from their sexuality.

THE UNANSWERED QUESTION: WHAT THEN, DO WE DO?

The religious messaging, thus far gives little support and guidance for Christians to be in their bodies, embrace their whole selves, and experience their sexuality in healthy ways. In a cultural landscape that sells and cheapens sex, there is confusion among Christians about how to *be*, sexually. For example, one woman told about the lack of guidance she had received in the church: "But they [the church leaders] ... never said what having a healthy sexuality could look like before you're married. Or that it was ok to think about it." She went on to say, "It was still something that I was really curious about. But I didn't know what to do with that curiosity."

Thankfully, we are not left merely with questions and destructive messages. The incarnation gives us the closest glimpse of holy sexuality and embodiment in the person of

Jesus Christ; God becoming flesh to accomplish the ultimate redemptive work is more than a mere nod to the "necessary evil" of our bodies. And, our sexual bodies seem to have a purpose that transcends (though it includes) the aim of procreation. In Christ, we have a roadmap for respect, empathy, and mutuality. The journey toward mutual, embodied sexuality in marriage has been shown to have spiritual fruit as well as relational fruit, as it enhances one's capacity to love and relate to God, others, and self.[11] While the legacy of the fall attacks the intimacy between man and woman, healthy sexuality can also be a vehicle for knowing God. In the following section, we offer a glimpse into engaging this journey of sexual wholeness and embodiment.

From Shame to Sexual Embodiment: The Journey

If our sexuality has the capacity to connect us with the divine and our partners, how then do we move from shame to a place of wholeness and embodiment? Brené Brown developed Shame Resilience Theory (SRT) to emphasize four ways to cultivate resilience to shame:[12] (1) become critically aware of the cultural and religious expectation and messages regarding our sexuality—such as the messages listed above; (2) develop self-awareness, and the ability to recognize and accept our own personal vulnerabilities to shame; (3) learn to "speak shame" or learn to voice our feelings of shame; and (4) form mutually empathic relationships that facilitate reaching out to others. Below we speak to these skills, integrating the comments of others' experiences.

CRITICALLY EVALUATING THE MESSAGES

One of the ways in which we develop resilience to shame is by critically evaluating the socio-cultural messages to which we are exposed.[13] One woman described how this process takes time:

> [We need to be] aware that sometimes we are stuck in our old belief systems, and that it is a journey—we can't just automatically replace old beliefs with new ones, even though we wish we could. [We] have to walk it out and be tough, and it's a lot of mindfulness and being able to notice what thoughts are present and how to challenge them, and encourage new ways of thinking.

Identifying and challenging negative beliefs about our sexuality is a process that requires time, energy, and self-compassion. It might be helpful to take some time and space to reflect on the messages that you remember hearing about your body and about your sexuality growing up. Some people find that journaling about their sexual development and experiences helps them understand the impact of these messages. Questions for this process are included at the conclusion of this chapter.

In addition to resisting negative messages, it is important to embrace positive, redemptive messages about sexuality. Church communities would benefit from having conversations that emphasize bodily-love, self-compassion, sexual safety, freedom, and responsible decision-making. Tina Schermer Sellers, a sex-therapist and researcher, advocates for a new "grace-filled" dialogue that highlights God's gift of sexual intimacy and desire within our homes and faith communities.[14] Focusing on the beauty and meaning of sex and sexuality creates openings for understanding that sex is *good*.

For example, one woman shared about how she used to understand sexuality as something that was "bad," "dirty," and "of the flesh" (meaning sinful). As she began to think about her sexuality in new ways, however, she resonated with the understanding that sexuality is about emotional, spiritual, and physical connection. In her words, "[through sex] I have a small glimpse of what God was intending in the beginning. Of wanting to be in this deep connection...I think that sex is such a beautiful thing." To her, sexual attraction and energy is a yearning to be totally reconnected with others. It is the closest expression of being able to fully know one another; through our sexuality, we come to a deeper understanding of how we can be connected with God and others. For her, these insights took time and space to process, but they transformed the way she experienced her sexuality in relationship with her husband, and as part of her spiritual journey.

SELF-AWARENESS

As described above, we develop shame when we feel we are failing to meet the expectations that we perceive others have placed on us. As we name and understand our experiences of sexual shame, we are better equipped to deal with it. One woman shared,

I think that I had to reach a pretty strong place of dissatisfaction with the shame, and with even recognizing an awareness of what was happening ... And [I] would pray about it a lot, and cry about it, and journal about it, and try to think about different strategies.

By actively engaging with her feelings of shame, she developed self-awareness and self-compassion.

Similarly, a man described to us how, because of the overwhelming silence about sexuality in his home and community, his sexual growth was "stunted." He found that learning about sexuality, and having the language for his sexual experiences promoted sexual responsibility, allowing him to connect with his sexuality in positive ways.

We can also develop greater self-awareness and understanding of our shame and shaming experiences by intentionally attuning to ourselves. Some people find that unpacking how shame manifests in their physical bodies is a helpful starting point in this process. When we feel shame, for example, we might avert our gaze, bow our heads, hunch our shoulders, blush, or cover our face.[15] By recognizing the bodily sensations we become more aware of shame in the moment. It is helpful to become aware of some of the thoughts that come up when you are feeling shame. For example, when experiencing sexual shame, some people might think "my body is disgusting" or "I am damaged goods." Recognizing that these voices are rooted in shame can help us choose to talk to ourselves in more loving and compassionate ways.

Developing self-awareness in relationship with one another is key to recognizing what our vulnerabilities to shame are. In our research, the men and women spoke about how they became aware of experiences that "triggered" their shame. For example, some spoke about how when their partner rejected their sexual advances they were "triggered" or overwhelmed. When they recognized this as a trigger, they became mindful of their body, their emotions, and their thoughts. This enabled them to slow down, and ask questions. In this case, they might have asked themselves, "Is my partner rejecting me (the shame voice), or is he/she simply tired?" or, "Does my partner find me unattractive, or is she/he under stress?" This developable skill, called mentalization, helps combat the shame voices that pull us away from mutual intimacy.

DEVELOPING EMPATHIC RELATIONSHIPS

We all need people in our lives with whom we can share our strengths and our struggles. Researchers studying attachment and neurodevelopment are finding that our brains are hard-wired for connection.[16] Opening ourselves to connection, however, can be difficult when we are grappling with shame. When painful feelings of shame are provoked, we tend to want to isolate and withdraw from relationships. Being authentically seen and known in the midst of shame is arguably the most powerful agent of healing. Brené Brown defines connection as, "the energy that exists between people when they feel seen, heard, and valued; when they can give and receive without judgment; and when they derive substance and strength from the relationship."[17] It is this type of connection that fosters resilience and helps people overcome sexual shame.

Telling our stories of shame is courageous. It also requires tenderness, and an ability to discern when to tell our stories with people who are able to meet us with openness and trust. Those who shared their stories said that connection with their partners, their communities, and with God was integral in this process of healing.

Partners. Cultivating open communication, mutual love, affirmation, and empathy in our marriages helps us feel safe to explore all parts of ourselves. Talking about our vulnerabilities is scary—especially when these vulnerabilities are related to topics that have been silenced in our religion and/or culture (e.g. sex). But, leaning into the discomfort of hard conversations deepens intimacy and fosters more fulfilling sexual experiences. One woman described this in her relationship with her husband:

> We talked so much around sex and around like, "can we try this," or "I felt kind of funny with that," or "I used to like that but I don't so much anymore." I think we push to talk about it when it feels uncomfortable and vulnerable because we care so much about it you know, in terms of marriage.

Rather than appeasing or disconnecting, they were able to share, be present, and love each other by continuing to have hard conversations. Their openness to, and acceptance of, each other enabled them to connect deeply.

When we share openly, we need to be received with gentleness, care, and empathy to feel safe. When someone is empathic to our feelings and experiences, it means that they, too, are open, vulnerable, and moved by what we say—they listen well and hold space for us.

Jennifer, one woman in our study, beautifully describes her internal transformation as she received her husband, Walter's empathy toward her. At first, Jennifer thought "he was full of crap" when Walter affirmed her beauty. She felt that it was impossible that he could actually love and enjoy her. Jennifer found that she disconnected from him in those moments, because she was disconnecting from herself. But it really hurt Walter to hear her say, "I just hate my body." sometimes he would cry in pain, and say to her "I wish you could just see who you are."

His persistence in caring for her, hurting with her, and actually seeing her beauty helped her. She began to see that her self-hatred was unloving towards him, because it broke their connection. When Jennifer empathized with Walter's pain she was able to return and care for her truer, deeper self. She could stop "torturing her body" and embrace herself and her sexuality. This story reflects a truth that was revealed in many other people's journeys: when we are deeply seen and empathized with, we move into deeper connection with ourselves and others.

Community While our relationship with our spouse can foster and support resilience to sexual shame, relationships with community are also a powerful force of healing. There is great beauty and meaning in mutual vulnerability in our friendships. Often a friend's vulnerability can open us up to deeper exposure and transformation.

For example, it was only after Mary's friend shared her own story of sexual shame that Mary felt safe enough to finally talk to someone about her shame. Mary found it deeply therapeutic to hear her friend validate her feelings, and say: "Yes! Of course you feel that way! It's ok to feel that way ... That does affect you...And that's still real and true." She spoke about how it felt "so much lighter" to release her shame and to be met with love and compassion. She recalls, "...that was really helpful, just to see truth instead of, when it's secretive, it's always so much bigger." By bringing her shame into the light, the power of its darkness could not be sustained. This story illustrates how being vulnerable with one another brings healing—when we are brave, and show ourselves and our stories to someone we can trust, it gives them the strength and courage to show themselves.

God. Our spirituality and our relationship with God is a significant source of healing and journeying toward wholeness. Shifting from a shaming, rules-based understanding of sexuality to an affirming, fully experienced sense of sexuality often takes place in the context of a relationship with God. When we are able to receive and experience the fullness of God's infinite grace and hear God's loving voice towards ourselves and our bodies, we are opened up to extend the same grace and love toward ourselves and others.

Interestingly, the way we experience God has a significant impact on our sexuality. Researchers have found that if a person believes that God is punitive, harsh and critical, they are more likely to have critical evaluations of their sexuality.[18] In our research, those who were able to receive the depth of love that God was offering them were able to see their sexuality as a gift.

For example, one man, who had, for years, experienced a profound sense of struggle with sexual addiction shared about a divine encounter with a loving God as deeply healing. He said that through this experience and others he learned that "God is all about sexuality and wants to get in the mess of it, the beauty of it, the darkness of it, and actually create something awesome that has no shame and is full of grace." For this man, this experience meant that God affirmed his sexuality as so deeply *good* that he desired to express it in ways that were honoring, safe, and loving. At the time of the interview he remained "sober" from his sex addiction and free from the shame of his past. Instead of turning toward his addiction, he was able to give and fully receive in his relationships with his wife and God.

Through encountering God's love, beauty, and affirmation of pleasure and desire, we begin to wholeheartedly embrace our sexuality as a symbol of intimacy with God. It might be helpful to take some time in prayer and journaling, and ask to hear how God sees you, your body, and your sexuality. By engaging with God, community and our partners, we journey toward an embodied sexual expression of deep connection and wholeness.

THE ROLE OF SEXUALITY IN MUTUALITY AND INTIMACY

We hope to have encouraged you with a vision that our bodies, specifically our sexuality, are integral to knowing and loving each other and to knowing and loving God. Jesus, who was fully man and fully God, revolutionizes and transforms the way that we approach our bodies, our spirits, our emotions, our relationships, and our sexuality. In a time of rigid separation of men and women, Jesus broke down barriers and modeled for us the possibility of wholeness and intimacy through embracing our physicality.

Our physicality is not somehow less important or less pure than our spirituality, but they are joined together in the relationships we live out with our partners. It is possible to live out our sexuality in an integrated and harmonious way, so that our spirituality enriches and gives meaning to our sexuality, and vice versa.[19] Interestingly, more and more researchers have begun to identify links between our religious and spiritual experiences and our sexuality. For example, some researchers have found that the perception that the sexual bond is sacred predicted increased marital satisfaction, sexual satisfaction, greater frequency of sexual activity, and greater sexual intimacy and spiritual intimacy in heterosexual newlywed couples.[20]

Another researcher, who explored the experiences and meaning of "profound sexual and spiritual encounters" of Christian couples, found common themes, including feeling a sense of awe and transcendence, experiencing God's presence, and feeling intense union with each other.[21] Through these sexual experiences, the couples experienced transformation and healing, empowerment and gender equality. These experiences represent a breakdown of dualism, and affirm that the body, soul, and spirit can intersect, resulting in "ecstatic bonding at new and wondrous heights."[22] The experience of integrating spirituality and sexuality breaks through the chains of patriarchy and shame, resulting in wholeness and connection with self and others.

ENGAGING SEXUALITY MEANINGFULLY IN YOUR MARRIAGE

To bring this chapter to its most practical focus, we invite you into a journey of engaging your sexuality meaningfully in your marriage. We invite you to hope with your partner for a sexual relationship that brings fulfilling awareness of being created for relationship, as you experience closeness in and through, rather than in spite of, your bodies. This is so much more than what is portrayed by Hollywood. And it is more complex than the view that following the rules of pre-marital abstinence results in perfect sexual "fireworks" upon marriage. In your sexual bond with your spouse, you have the opportunity to give each other the gift of being naked and unashamed, of loving and being loved, and seeking God in the vulnerable life-affirming intimacy of marital sexuality.

QUESTIONS FOR INDIVIDUAL REFLECTION AND/OR GROUP DISCUSSION

Reviewing the themes we have explored so far, we invite you to consider your sexual journey, and to map out where you want to grow. As a sexual being, the way you experience yourself and your sexuality is unique. What do you bring to the table in your views and experience of your sexuality in your own body? Being seen and known in empathic relationships with others, with one's partner, and with God, is a vital part of embracing fulfilled sexuality. This journey takes time and the questions below are prompts to begin a discussion and reflection. We expect some questions for discussion can be life-giving in safe, small group formats while others may be most helpful for individual reflection, or for consideration with one's partner.

GENERAL QUESTIONS

- Considering your unique experiences as a sexual being, what messages, positive and negative, have you internalized throughout your life?
- How did people in your family of origin express love and affection with each other? What was communicated about modesty, developing sexuality, and sexual behavior? How did your parents approach sex education? Were you exposed to games with sexual themes or erotic material (such as pornography) as a child?

- Can you identify contradictory messages that you have implicitly accepted about gender and sexuality? What are the cultural values you have learned about sexuality? What religious messages have you learned? How do you make sense of the contradictory messages that you have heard?
- What was your view of sex as a child? How has your view of sex changed over your life? How would you describe it today?
- Have you experienced shame in your sexuality? If so, how did you experience it in your body, in your sexuality and in your relationships?

QUESTIONS SPECIFICALLY RECOMMENDED FOR COUPLES

- Describe your earliest experiences with sexual attraction.
- What is your dating history? Which relationships have been most significant in shaping your experience of yourself as a man or woman? What have your experiences been with kissing, petting, oral sex, and coitus?
- To what extent have you been exposed to and used erotic material or pornography?
- How have you experienced physical, sexual, or emotional abuse?
- What are your expectations and fears about your sexual life, currently? Describe your sexual fantasy life.
- How does your spiritual life relate to your sexual life?
- How do you hope to grow in your sexuality?

- How do you know what feels safe, free, and loving for you in sexual expression?

Practical Exercises

The following two exercises are offered to promote embodied experiencing and intimacy.

Experiencing Your Own Nakedness

For this exercise, we encourage you to spend a period of time naked. You decide how long—for some, five minutes is just right while others may continue this exercise for an hour. For many people, this is an unusual practice. After all, nakedness is often restricted to bathing and sex. During this exercise, practice non-judgmentally noticing of every part of your body from your hair down to your feet. Don't just notice appearance, but notice how it feels to be in each part of your body and to experience the world through each part of your body. Do some parts feel more important to being you than others? Can you stretch your imagination to reflect on being yourself even in your little toe? Notice your body's strength to hold you, notice if you experience pain or tension anywhere, and try to express self-acceptance and appreciation for this body that gives you access to the world.

To further this embodied experiencing to a spiritual relational exercise, practice being aware of the gaze of your creator God as you notice your nakedness. Allow yourself to listen prayerfully for the affirmation of the one who knitted your body together. Be aware of the approval, the love, the intimate knowing of God towards your whole being. Allow the physical nakedness to represent literally and metaphorically that you are seen and known by the Creator. In this exercise, you may experience uncomfortable feelings and reactions; if so, don't worry about them, just notice and let them be. Most importantly, listen for God's voice of love. This exercise can be repeated and deepened as the uncomfortable feelings and reactions diminish and one's body-awareness and appreciation deepens in dialogue with the loving Creator.

Sensate Focus for Couples

Sensate Focus is a common component of sex therapy where partners take turns with the "active" and "passive" roles and practice sensual and intimate expression without intercourse. For this exercise, you should have at least thirty minutes available in a private space. The "passive" partner is responsible for focusing his or her attention on the sensations felt when being caressed by the partner, even allowing oneself to be "selfish" in this enjoyment. The "active" partner is responsible to caress the passive partner gently all over his/her body, excluding erogenous zones (the parts of the body that can be stimulated for sexual arousal such as the breasts, genitals, inner thighs, and mouth).

For this exercise, both partners are nude. The passive partner starts by lying on his/her stomach while the active partner caresses him or her in ways that are pleasurable. There is no "right way" to do this, but the passive partner can share what feels pleasurable as well as express if there is any area s/he does not like to be touched. The active partner starts at the back of the neck, ears, and works all the way down to the buttocks, legs, and feet, using his/her hands and/or lips to caress the passive partner. The active partner focuses on how it feels to touch the passive partner's body, noticing what they enjoy and appreciate about the partner's body. After the head-to-toe sweep is completed, the passive partner may then roll onto his/her back and the active partner caresses the front side of the body, still avoiding the erogenous zones.

During this time, the passive partner focuses his/her attention on the sensation of being caressed, trying not to think about anything else, even about whether the active partner may be getting tired. In the exercise of sensate focus, the passive partner's job is to focus on this experience of being pleasured, telling the partner how it feels, how the pressure is, or feedback about the pacing. Don't talk too much with words during this exercise as the focus is on attuning to your own and each other's sensations.

Either during the same practice session or another time soon after, the couple switches positions, taking the opposite role of "active" and "passive" partner and repeat the exercise. After several times of practicing this non-demand touch, erogenous zones can be included in the exercise, but couples are encouraged to practice it without leading to intercourse. The primary goal is to expand the repertoire of sensual touch and intimacy in a way that is safe, mutually satisfying, and is not focused on genital intercourse and orgasm, which often become the sole focus of sexuality.

Through and within our bodies, in mutual intimacy, we can experience safety, freedom, pleasure, and connection. We wish for you to experience increasing joy and love in your sexual lives as you deepen your self-understanding and seek grace, self-acceptance, and fulfillment in God's love.

RECOMMENDED FOR FURTHER READING

Rekindling Desire by Barry McCarthy and Emily McCarthy. New York: Taylor and Francis, 2014.

Embracing the Body: Finding God in Our Flesh and Bone by Tara Owens. Downers Grove: IVP Books, 2015.

The Heart of Desire: Keys to the Pleasures of Love by Stella Resnick. New York: Wiley, 2012.

A Celebration of Sex: A Guide to Enjoying God's Gift of Sexual Intimacy by Douglas Rosenau. Nashville: Thomas Nelson, 2002.

Sex for Christians: The Limits and Liberties of Sexual Living (Rev. Ed.) by Lewis Smedes. Grand Rapids: W. E. Eerdmans, 1994.

What About...

– 7 –

What about Headship?

From Hierarchy to Equality

Philip B. Payne

In Christ, there is no male-female division (Galatians 3:28; 1 Corinthians 11:11). Jesus and Paul teach a radically new way to live together in love and mutual submission, a way that I can testify leads to peace, joy, and maturity for both partners. In contrast, marriages modeled on male headship tend to inhibit the free exchange of ideas between equals that develops maturity in wives and husbands. It is simply not natural in close friendships for one friend always to have the final authority in decision making. How would you feel if your best friend told you that henceforth you would always have to submit to his or her authority? Would it promote the growth of your friendship? Would it promote the maturity of both friends? No, and perhaps that's why both Jesus and Paul affirm close personal relationships of mutual respect and self-giving.

I grew up in a loving Christian home where Dad was the head of the house. But something happened in 1973 that made me examine what Scripture teaches about man and woman. When I was beginning my PhD studies in New Testament at the University of Cambridge, I was shocked to hear a lecturer state: "There is no passage in the New Testament that limits the ministry of women." I almost shouted, "That's not true!" I determined to prove him wrong. But after months examining the New Testament in Greek, I had to admit he was right: the New Testament never clearly limits women's ministry, but clearly affirms women's ministry many times.

Even after this discovery, however, I still thought the Bible gave husbands final authority in the home. I insisted that my wife include submission to me in her marriage vows. I thought I was justified in this for two key reasons, both from Ephesians 5. First, Ephesians 5:24 teaches, "Now as the church submits to Christ, so also wives should submit to their husbands in everything." Second, Ephesians 5:23 says, "For the husband is the head of the wife as Christ is the head of the church, his body, of which he is the Savior" (NIV). The meaning of these seemed obvious—that a wife must submit to her husband in everything and that a husband is the head with authority over his wife.

Closer investigation of Scripture, however, led me to discover that these passages do not support male leadership in marriage, but teach mutual submission and self-giving in marriage. Part of the problem is the legacy of translations such as the NIV, RSV, NRSV, and ESV, which conceal how Paul defined "head" in verse 23 and incorrectly split the sentence including Ephesians 5:21–24 into two separate paragraphs. [Another issue is failing to interpret Scripture as a united whole and instead picking and choosing verses to fit one's favored view] As we consider together the original language of the

New Testament, we will discover clear affirmations of mutual submission in marriage.

MUTUAL SUBMISSION IN MARRIAGE

Before examining the notion of male headship in marriage, let us consider three key scriptural teachings challenging the idea that "wives should submit to their husbands in everything." First, wives should not submit to their husbands when asked to sin. It is clear from Acts 5:8–10 that Sapphira was dead wrong to agree with her husband Ananias. She was not submitting "as the church submits to Christ," for Christ would never call us to "lie to the Holy Spirit!" Consequently, "as the church submits to Christ" is a crucial qualifier that frees wives from submitting to anything Christ prohibits.

Second, *mutual* submission is the explicit context of Ephesians 5:21–33. Paul does not give any command here that applies only to husbands or only to wives. Early church fathers also insisted that submission in the body of Christ is truly mutual, applying to all, even bishops.[1] Origen, Jerome, and Chrysostom confirmed that the wife's submission is one facet of mutual submission.[2] Mutual submission between husband and wife is both putting themselves at the disposal of the other. It is, according to the most reliable Greek lexicon, mutual "voluntary yielding in love" (BDAG 1042).

The context for Ephesians 5:23 starts at verse 18, where Paul commands all believers, "be filled with the Holy Spirit." He describes how to live a Spirit-filled life with a series of parallel commands in one long Greek sentence. The last command is found in verses 21-22: "submitting to one another out of reverence for Christ, wives to your own husbands as to the Lord, for ...."

The earliest Greek manuscripts show no verb "submit" in verse 22.[3] So, even though verse 22 is often translated as "Wives, submit to your husbands ..." in reality, the verb "submit" is only found in verse 21. This shows that verse 22 is linked to and applies verse 21's direction to submit to "one another out of reverence to Christ."

Third, the Bible affirms the equal rights and obligations of man and woman in marriage. Paul's longest and most detailed treatment of marriage is in 1 Corinthians 7. This passage never implies the husband's leadership or that husbands and wives should have different roles. It identifies exactly the same rights and responsibilities for wives and husbands regarding twelve different issues about marriage, both natural and spiritual. Symmetrically balanced wordings emphasize the equality of men and women:

> 7:2 "Let each man have his own wife, and let each woman have her own husband."
>
> 7:3 "Let the husband fulfill his marital duty to his wife, and likewise the wife to her husband."
>
> 7:4 "The wife does not have authority over her own body, but her husband does. In the same way, the husband does

not have authority over his own body, but his wife does."

7:5 "Do not deprive each other except by mutual consent."

7:10–11 "A wife must not separate[4] from her husband ... and a husband must not leave his wife."[5]

7:12–13 "If any brother has a wife who is not a believer and she is willing to live with him, he must not leave her. And if a woman has a husband who is not a believer and he is willing to live with her, she must not leave him."

7:14 "For the unbelieving husband has been sanctified through his wife, and the unbelieving wife has been sanctified through her husband."

7:15 "But if the unbeliever separates ... the believing brother or sister is not bound."

7:16 "How do you know, wife, whether you will save your husband? Or how do you know, husband, whether you will save your wife?

7:28 "But if you do marry, you have not sinned; and if a virgin marries, she has not sinned."

7:32, 34b "An unmarried man is concerned about the Lord's affairs—how he can please the Lord. . . . An unmarried woman or virgin is concerned about the Lord's affairs: Her aim is to be devoted to the Lord in both body and spirit."

7:33–34a, 34c "But a married man is concerned about the affairs of this world—how he can please his wife—and his interests are divided. . . . But a married woman is concerned about the affairs of this world—how she can please her husband."

The striking egalitarian dynamics of marriage expressed throughout this passage are without parallel in the literature of the ancient world, which viewed marriage as hierarchical.[6] Bible scholar Richard Hays, observeing how revolutionary this was writes, ["Paul offers a paradigm-shattering vision of marriage as a relationship in which the partners are bonded together in submission to one another."[7]]

A fundamental principle for Bible study is to interpret passages in harmony with other passages by the same author. Furthermore, since God is the ultimate author of the original text of Scripture, we need to interpret passages in light of clear teaching throughout the Bible. One should reject any hierarchical interpretation that contradicts the clear teaching of the equal rights and responsibilities of husband and wife affirmed in 1 Corinthians 7.

WHAT DOES PAUL MEAN BY, "A HUSBAND IS HEAD OF HIS WIFE"?

Having demonstrated that Paul does not teach the idea of one-sided submission of the wife to the husband, let us consider male headship in marriage. I had thought, like most English readers, that ["the husband is head of his wife" teaches that the husband has a position of authority over his wife and the final say in family decisions.] Decades of study of Greek usage of "head" showed me I was wrong about this, too. Practically, as well, I discovered that my assuming headship was often toxic to the health of our marriage. In contrast, the practice of mutual submission has strengthened our marriage partnership.

My understanding of this passage gradually changed as I examined the structure of its argument and the meaning of its words in Greek. Following is my own translation of Ephesians 5:18–32 closely reflecting its text in the earliest Greek manuscripts. English words with no direct Greek equivalent are in italics.

> Do not get drunk with wine, which leads to debauchery. Instead, be filled with *the* Spirit, speaking to one another with psalms, hymns, and songs from *the* Spirit, singing and making music from your heart to the Lord, giving thanks always for everything in *the* name of our Lord Jesus Christ to God *the* Father, submitting to one another out of reverence for Christ, wives to your own husbands as to the Lord, for a husband is "head" of *his* wife as also Christ is "head" of the church in the sense that he is savior of the body *through giving himself in love for the body.* Now as the church submits to Christ, so also wives *should submit* to their husbands in everything.[8]

> Husbands, love *your* wives, just as also Christ loved the church and gave himself up for her in order to make her holy, cleansing *her* by the washing of water in *accordance with the* divine teachings,"[9] and to present her to himself as the radiant church, not having stain or

wrinkle or any other blemish, but holy and blameless. In this same way, husbands ought to love their own wives as their own bodies. He who loves his own wife loves himself. After all, no one ever hated their own body, but feeds and cherishes it, just as Christ *does* the church—for we are members of his body. "For this reason a man will leave *his* father and mother and be united to his wife, and the two will become one flesh." This is a profound mystery—but I am talking about Christ and the church. However, this is also essential: each one of you must love his wife as he loves himself, and the wife respect her husband.

Paul explains this passage as primarily about Christ and the church in verse 32. Reference to marriage begins in verse 22 as an illustration of submitting to one another out of reverence for Christ, and Paul refers in almost every verse to Christ and the church.

"Headship"

Before going further, let us pause to consider what we mean by "headship." *Webster's New World Dictionary* represents typical English usage, and most English dictionaries, by defining "headship" as, "the position or authority of a chief or leader; leadership; command." Many assume that Ephesians 5 teaches the husband's headship over his wife, but the word "headship" never occurs anywhere in the Bible.

Since a husband is not physically the "head" of his wife, all scholars agree that "head" here is a metaphor. In English, "leader," is the most common metaphorical meaning for "head," as in "head of the company." Many English readers know the expression "the husband is the head of the family" (which is not in the Bible) and assume that Paul taught that the husband is "head" of the wife in the sense of having authority over her. But is this how Paul's Greek contemporaries would have understood "head"?

According to Swiss theologian Markus Barth, Ephesians 5:23 is the first known reference to a husband as "'head of his wife' [so it] must be understood as original with the author of Ephesians."[10] If Barth is correct, Paul was coining a fresh metaphor, so we ought to ask what he intended in the context of Ephesians 5 and what established Greek meaning of "head" best fits here. After extensive research, many respected Greek scholars have concluded that "head" here does not imply "headship" in the English sense of "the position or authority of a chief or leader." In light of Paul's other teachings about marriage, it is crucial to examine Greek usage of "head" and Paul's use of "head" elsewhere.

"HEAD" IN DICTIONARIES OF GREEK USAGE UP TO THE NEW TESTAMENT

Greek use of the word "head" is summarized in the most exhaustive Greek dictionary, called "LSJ."[11] LSJ lists forty-eight figurative meanings for "head," but does not list "leader," "authority," or anything related as a meaning for "head."[12]

Virtually all secular Greek dictionaries covering usage up to the time of the New Testament do not give even one example of the Greek word for head (*kephale*) that implies authority.[13] The most exhaustive New Testament dictionary concludes that in secular usage, this word "is not employed for the head of a society. This is first found in the sphere of the Greek Old Testament."[14]

"*Head*" *in the Greek translation of the Old Testament*

The word for "head" conveys "leader" in the Hebrew Scriptures 171 times.[15] The NASB, a literal English translation, reflects common English metaphorical use of "head" to convey "leader" by translating 115 of these 171 instances "head."[16] Yet the standard Greek Old Testament used in churches in Paul's day, known as the LXX, uses the Greek word for "head" (*kephale*) clearly as a metaphor meaning "leader" only once.[17] The almost complete absence of "head" as a metaphor for "leader" in the LXX demonstrates that the LXX translators, like most Greek dictionaries, did not recognize *kephale* as a natural metaphor for "leader" in Greek. If it were natural in Greek to convey "leader" using the word "head" as a metaphor, we would expect the LXX to translate most of these 171 instances of the Hebrew word "head" meaning "leader" with "head" (*kephale*), but they do not, even though they almost always (in 226 of 239 instances) chose *kephale* to translate this same Hebrew word when it means a physical "head."

The sharp contrast between the abundant use of "head" as a metaphor for "leader" in Hebrew and English and only one clear instance in the LXX is especially striking for two reasons. First, it goes against the LXX translators' tendency to translate Hebrew words with the closest Greek equivalent. We know *kephale* was the closest Greek equivalent from their overwhelming use of *kephale* to translate this same Hebrew word when it refers to a literal head. Second, it is abundantly well documented in the LXX for "Greek words to extend their range of meaning in an un-Greek way after the Hebrew word they render."[18] The fact that in spite of this tendency, there is only one clear instance where a LXX translator used *kephale* as a metaphor for "leader" shows that *kephale* did not naturally convey "leader" in Greek.

This is important since it warns us not to assume that when Paul spoke of Christ as "head" of the church or a husband as "head" of his wife that he meant "leader" or that he was implying an authority structure. In fact, this meaning was so foreign to Greek that even when "head" was the most obvious translation choice for "head" in Hebrew, the LXX translators almost never use "head" as a metaphor[19] for "leader."

To summarize, both secular Greek dictionaries and the standard Greek translation of the Scriptures used by Paul and in the churches give strong evidence that "leader" was not a natural Greek meaning for "head." Only if Paul clearly explained that by "head" he meant "leader" would his readers be likely to recognize that meaning. Consequently, we should be wary lest we read the English meaning "leader" into Paul's uses of "head." Indeed, we should expect a different meaning than "leader" when Paul uses "head" as a metaphor.

OBJECTIVE CRITERIA FOR DETERMINING WHAT "HEAD" MEANS IN EPHESIANS 5:23

Standard principles of interpretation provide three objective grounds to decide what meaning Paul intended by "head" in Ephesians 5:23:

1. The gold standard principle asks, "Did the author define the meaning of this word in this context?" Authors often do this by adding a parallel phrase that substitutes a different word to explain their intended meaning. This is called "apposition."
2. Is there anything in the literary context in addition to the author's definition that explains what the word means or conflicts with proposed meanings?
3. How does the author use this word elsewhere, especially in similar contexts?

When these principles are applied to Ephesians 5:23, all three support that "head" means "savior" in the sense of "source of love and nourishment."

PRINCIPLE 1: PAUL DEFINES "HEAD" AS "SOURCE" IN COLOSSIANS 1:18 AND "SAVIOR" IN EPHESIANS 5:23

Twice Paul defines what he means by *kephale* by using apposition, a parallel phrase that substitutes a word to explain what he means by "head." Colossians 1:18: "he is the head (*kephale*) of the body, the church, who is the *arche*," the "origin" (NEB) or "the source of the body's life" (TEV).[20] Verses 20–22 twice explains that Christ became the source of the church by "making peace by the blood of his cross ... in his body of flesh by his death."

Paul defines "head" in Ephesians 5:23 as "savior" in the sense of "source of love and nourishment": "For the husband is head of the wife as

| Christ [is] | head | of the | church |
| he | savior | of the | body" |

| ho Christos | kephale | tes | ekklesias |
| autos | soter | tou | somatos[21] |

Paul goes on to explain what Christ did as savior of the body: "Christ loved the church and gave himself up for her" and "nourishes and cherishes" her. As head, Christ is the church's savior, its *source* of love and nourishment. Similarly, husbands as "head" are to "love your wives just as Christ loved the church and gave himself up for her" and to "nourish and cherish" them "just as Christ does the church"). "Head" is a natural metaphor for "source" since the head is the source through which the body receives nourishment, breath, sight, hearing, smelling, and taste. One can even say that as Christ is the source of life for the church, the husband, in that culture, was the source of life for his wife since he provided all that was essential for her to live.

The aspect of "head" that this passage develops is a call for husbands to love, give themselves for, nourish, and cherish their wives just as Christ as "head" is the source of all these for the church. This passage does not call husbands to have authority over their wives, but rather "to submit to one another," a command to the whole church that Paul specifically applies first to wives in verses 22–24 and then to husbands in verses 25–33. The ways Paul commands husbands to submit to their wives are by loving them, giving themselves for them, nourishing them, and cherishing them.

Translation matters ✗ Many Bible versions correctly preserve Paul's apposition explaining "head" as "savior."[22] It is tragic, however, that many popular English translations conceal this apposition. Some versions insert "and," which gives the false impression that these are two independent statements (KJV, RSV, ESV). Others add "of which" giving the false impression that the second parallel phrase refers only to the church (NRSV, NIV) rather than explaining the meaning of "head." A few add punctuation and change the word order, which completely conceals the original parallel structure and apposition (RSV, ESV). Some versions capitalize "Savior" (RSV, ESV), making it seem like a title instead of an explanation of the meaning of "head."[23]

PRINCIPLE 2: IS THERE ANYTHING ELSE IN THE CONTEXT THAT EXPLAINS WHAT THE WORD MEANS?

In addition to Paul's explanation that "head" means savior in the sense of source of love and nourishment, "head" also means "source" in the preceding chapter:

> "Instead, speaking the truth in love, we will grow to become in every respect the mature body of him who is the **head**, that is, Christ. **From him** the whole body, joined and held together by every supporting ligament, **grows** and builds itself up in love, as each part does its work" (Ephesians 4:15–16 NIV, emphasis added).

Christ is the "head ... from whom ... the body grows" affirms that Christ is the source of the body's growth. "From" implies "source." This passage is an original inspiration. Nowhere does the Old Testament speak of Israel as "members of God's body."[24] This prepares the reader to understand "head" as source in chapter 5.

Furthermore, as we saw above, mutual submission is the explicit context of Ephesians 5:21–24. This is incompatible with interpreting "head" as establishing a hierarchy in which only the wife must be submissive to her husband, not vice versa.

PRINCIPLE 3: HOW DOES THE AUTHOR USE THE WORD ELSEWHERE?

"Head" meaning "source" is supported not only in the

preceding chapter (4:15–16) but also in other passages by Paul, including Colossians 2:19, "the head, from[25] whom the whole body ... grows." "Source" makes good sense as the meaning of nine[26] of Paul's eleven metaphorical uses of *kephale*, whereas not even one instance has been demonstrated to mean "authority over."[27]

All three principles clearly support that "head" in Ephesians 5:23 means "savior" in the sense of "source of love and nourishment." Based on a clear understanding of Paul's language and intent in Ephesians 5, how does he instruct husbands and wives to live out their marriage relationship as followers of Jesus?

DOES EPHESIANS 5 TEACH THAT CHRIST IS THE MODEL FOR THE HUSBAND ONLY, NOT HIS WIFE?

No. In Ephesians 5:2, Paul commands the whole church, including wives, "walk in the way of love, just as Christ loved us and gave himself up for us." Ephesians 4:13 expresses the goal that we all attain "to the whole measure of the fullness of Christ." Paul doesn't ask husbands to do anything more than this.

DOES PAUL COMMAND ONLY THE HUSBAND TO LOVE HIS WIFE, NOT THE REVERSE?

No. Titus 2:4 explicitly calls women "to love their husbands."

DOES EPHESIANS 5 TEACH THAT AS CHRIST HAS AUTHORITY OVER THE CHURCH, A HUSBAND SHOULD HAVE AUTHORITY OVER HIS WIFE?

Christ has authority over the church, but that is not Paul's point in any of his depictions of Christ as "head" of the church. Whenever Paul refers to Christ as "head of the church" he does this to affirm that Christ is the source of growth, life, love, nourishment, or purity of the church (Ephesians 4:15; 5:23–33; Colossians 1:18–22; 2:19). Analogies always break down when a divine-human relationship is compared to a human-human relationship. Accordingly, Paul concludes in Ephesians 5:32, "This is a profound mystery, but I am speaking about Christ and the church." The key point of the analogy Paul stresses again and again is: "love your wives as Christ loved the church." He never says the husband has authority over his wife, and certainly not that the husband has authority corresponding to the authority Christ has over the church. That would deify husbands! Chrysostom vehemently denies that husbands have authority like Christ.[28] If Paul taught male leadership in the home, why does 1 Timothy 5:14 call wives to "rule their homes," literally "be house despots" (oikodespotein)?

DOES EPHESIANS 5 TEACH THAT WIVES MUST SUBMIT TO THEIR HUSBANDS IN EVERYTHING?

Ephesians 5:24's implicit command, "wives should submit to your husbands in everything" is specifically qualified by and depends for its verb on: "as the church submits to Christ." It is only "as the church submits to Christ" that wives are called to submit to their husbands. As noted above, God judged Sapphira worthy of death for submitting to her husband Ananias, by agreeing to lie (Acts 5:1–11). First Samuel 25 praises Abigail for not submitting to her husband, Nabal.

DOES EPHESIANS 5–6 COMMAND SUBMISSION OF WIVES TO HUSBANDS, CHILDREN TO PARENTS, AND SLAVES TO MASTERS, GIVING THEM ALL AS EXAMPLES OF SUBMITTING TO ONE ANOTHER?

Paul's commands to masters to "do the same to" their slaves in Ephesians 6:9 and "grant justice and equality (or fairness) to your slaves" in Colossians 4:1 may imply mutual submission, but they are grammatically unrelated to "submitting to one another." Nothing in Paul's commands to children and fathers implies mutual submission, nor are they grammatically linked to "submitting to one another." Twelve verses separate the commands to children from "submitting to one another." Neither the passage about slaves or children contain any form of the word "submit."

In the original text of Ephesians 5 "submit" occurs only twice: "submitting to one another" and "as the church submits to Christ," never following the subject "wives." These instances of "submit" provide the context (mutual submission) and limit submission by wives to their husbands to "as the church submits to Christ." Some versions incorrectly create a paragraph break between 5:21 and 22, which butchers Paul's sentence and makes readers think verse 21 introduces the three following pairs.

Mutual submission introduces the wife's submission and sets the stage for Paul's culturally radical commands to husbands to "love your wives just as Christ loved the church and gave himself up for her" (5:25). Such love entails a husband's submission to his wife and respect for his wife. Accordingly, Paul makes no distinction between the obedience and honor children owe to their father than they owe to their mother in Ephesians 6:1–2. There is no "boss" in a marriage; husband and wife are equals.

Conclusion

On close examination, the New Testament neither requires one-way submission in marriage nor does it give one partner supremacy in decision-making. Paul's most extensive passage about marriage, 1 Corinthians 7, affirms the equal standing of husband and wife in twelve areas.

Paul commands all believers to submit to one another in Ephesians 5:21. The reciprocal pronoun "to one another" demands that the submission is reciprocal, going both ways. It is explicitly in the context of mutual submission that Paul adds to this same sentence, "wives to your own husbands," which depends for its verb on verse 21's "submitting to one another." Verses 22–24 combined with Paul's following commands to husbands—to love, give themselves for, nourish, and cherish their wives—express the reciprocity of mutual submission in marriage. Both husband and wife are to subordinate their desires in deference for the best for the other, putting themselves at the disposal of the other.

Submission is voluntary yielding in love.

Hardly any dictionaries of Greek usage up to the time of the New Testament list any instance where "head" means anything like "leader" or "authority," but many include "source." In Ephesians 5:23, Paul defines what he means by "head" as "savior": "Christ head of the church, he savior of the body." He then explains that as "head/savior" Christ is the church's *source* of love and nourishment, just as husbands should be for their wives (5:25, 29). The context of mutual submission conflicts with interpreting "head" to imply that a husband is in authority over his wife. "Head" meaning "source" in Ephesians 4:15–16 supports "head" conveying "source" in 5:23, as does Paul's usual use of "head" elsewhere. Nine of Paul's eleven metaphorical uses of "head" (*kephale*) make sense meaning "source." Paul's explanation of a husband being "head" of his wife mentions nothing about his having authority over her, but stresses his self-giving nourishing love for her modeled on Christ, the source of love and nourishment for the church.

Paul consistently affirms the equal standing and mutual submission of wife and husband. Paul does not limit roles based on gender. He encourages husband and wife to relate as equals who put each other's needs first. His focus is not on who's in charge but on how best to show love to each other. As Christ gave his life for us, we are to live our lives for one another.

QUESTIONS FOR DISCUSSION AND REFLECTION

1. What does it look like to submit to one another?
2. How does rethinking the meaning of head as "source" instead of "leader" change your perspective on this passage?
3. What else did you learn from this chapter and how might it impact your marriage?

– 8 –

What about Abuse?
Abuse and Church Theology

Nancy Murphy

MY STORY

The first time my husband hit me, I turned to the Scriptures for guidance. Growing up in the Christian faith and with a love for God, it made the most sense for me. He went for a walk, and as I huddled up in a ball, remembered verses that I had memorized as a girl:

> Wives, in the same way submit yourselves to your own husbands so that, if any of them do not believe the word, they may be won over without words by the behavior of their wives, when they see the purity and reverence of your lives (1 Pet. 3:1–2).

Searching my mind, additional verses surfaced regarding suffering and forgiveness:

> Who is going to harm you if you are eager to do good? But even if you should suffer for what is right, you are blessed. "Do not fear their threats; do not be frightened" (1 Pet. 3:13–14).

Be kind and compassionate to one another, forgiving each other, just as in Christ God forgave you (Eph. 4:32)

The "love chapter," as 1 Corinthians 13 has often been called, had been read at our wedding less than a week before. It says, in part: [love] keeps no record of wrongs (1 Cor. 13:5).

I silently recited my wedding vows, looking for direction in the words, "for better or worse, in sickness and health, for richer or poorer, 'til death parts us." Well I wasn't dead, and as far as I could tell, the Scriptures were clear that I was to continue to be submissive, that suffering was a part of God's redemptive plan, and regardless of how I was being treated, I was to be kind, tenderhearted, loving, and forgiving.

Reeling from the pain of being hit in the face and called names, yet spiritually resolute to be a wife my husband could trust and count on, I silenced my heartache and carried on as a "good wife" and a "good Christian." I hoped this would be the only time I was hit, but it was not. There were times I didn't fold his jeans the right way, or meals weren't prepared to his liking. Sometimes he had had a bad day at work and didn't feel I was being understanding enough. Once he acted out for no good reason, he just wanted to remind me who was boss. There always seemed to be a lesson he was trying to teach me.

I was open to making the changes I needed to in order to

stop making my husband so upset. He felt that I was making his life miserable and was hopeful for some direction as well. For my birthday, I asked my husband if we could meet with our pastor to tell him what was going on in our marriage. He agreed and set up a meeting. It seemed natural to turn to our pastor and his wife for help as the church had a longstanding reputation for supporting marriage and denouncing divorce. It felt like a safe first step. We went together to our pastor's home for dinner. After a nice meal together we began to open up to our pastor and his wife in their living room. I felt uncomfortable talking about being hit. I had forgiven my husband and felt that it was unwise to bring it up as it could stir up conflict. It was embarrassing to admit anything and somehow, even though the words were on the tip of my tongue, I held them in. My husband also stayed silent. When the pastor asked us what was on our minds, we simply smiled and alluded to our first year of marriage being harder than we had anticipated. Immediately, both our pastor and his wife broke out into laughter. They told us stories from their difficult first year and relayed stories of others who had also experienced unexpected adjustments. They assured us that this was common and we enjoyed dessert together as each of us tactfully avoided getting into any of the details.

Walking to our vehicle that evening, my husband tenderly took my hand, and told me he had really enjoyed our evening together. He thanked me for not saying more than I needed to and promised things would be different from now on. It was such a kind gesture and I so badly wanted to believe him, but I felt his words were like a paper boat being launched out on the ocean—a ship that floats for moments, but is inevitably taken down by the waves of life. Nothing had changed for us really. We had shared a nice meal, but we had not been able to speak freely. It wasn't safe. I left certain that our pastor and his wife were ill equipped for marriage—their own, as well as ours.

For 10 years, I circled the biblical texts I knew so well, looking for direction. Concordances led me to passages denouncing sexual immorality, divorce, and remarriage. I found passages for single people and widows, but none regarding violence and abuse. None of the pastors or Bible study leaders I knew directly said that abuse or violence in the home was right, but they would often direct their correctional teaching towards the one who was experiencing the abuse. It sounded something like this:

- Wives... let your husbands have time and space when they come home from work before you bring them your cares and concerns of your day.
- Wives... you have more words than your husbands. He may have used up his words all day at work and come home tired. Don't expect more of him than he is able to give.
- Wives... if you fulfill your husband's God-given sexual desires in ways that give him deep pleasure, he is more likely to be faithful.

- Wives... you know that sometimes you can be more emotional than is necessary.
- Wives... Scripture is clear that you can be given over to much talk, be careful you do not bring your husband down with your tongue.
- Wives... don't let yourselves go. You don't want to give Satan a foothold in your marriage.
- Wives... the Proverbs 31 woman brings her husband good, not harm, all the days of her life.... charm is deceptive, and beauty is fleeting, but a woman who fears the Lord is to be praised.

Scripture has been misused and/or misinterpreted to suggest that coercion and violence may be acceptable or even God's will. But God is a God of love, compassion, forgiveness, and justice with no tolerance for violence and oppression. "Give up your violence and oppression and do what is just and right," commands Ezekiel 45:9. The righteous avoid the ways of the violent. (Psa. 17:4). The New Testament instructs us not to put a violent person in a position of leadership in the church. (1 Tim. 3:3, Tit. 1:7) Anger is often used as justification for violence or controlling behavior, but the Scripture admonishes us to not sin when we are angry. (Eph. 4:26). Discord, jealousy, fits of rage, and selfish ambition are all named as acts of the sinful nature (Gal. 5:20). Instead we are called to bear the fruit of the Spirit; love, peace, patience, kindness, goodness, faithfulness, gentleness, and self-control (Gal.5:22).

When the church is silent on these issues, it contributes through bad theology to violence. Indirectly or directly, the church conveys that it is okay to be a dictator or tyrant in the home. As a result, many suffer in fear and silence as I and my children did, often hiding behind a public image of perfection or a family with disproportionate mental health issues such as anxiety or depression.

For those met with silence regarding their treatment within the marriage relationship, or at the hands of a parent, the internalized messages become, "If I do something better or different, the violence or abuse will no longer happen. This is about something that is wrong with me!"

As it turns out, domestic violence is a problem within the abuser, NOT with the one who is being abused. Only when the abuser begins to take responsibility for their own feelings, thoughts, and actions, can anything change.

Still searching for a way to be happily married, I found a book in the Christian bookstore entitled, *In the Name of Submission: A Painful Look at Wife Battering*, by Kay Marshall Strom. As I purchased this book, I told the cashier that it was for a friend. I blushed with shame as she read the cover before she put it in the bag.

As I read through this small book on an especially difficult night, I read:

- You are an important and worthwhile person.

- You deserve to be safe from fear and injury, especially in your own home.
- You deserve to be treated with respect.
- You are not to blame for being beaten and abused. You are not the cause of your partner's violent behavior.
- No one has the right to accuse you of liking or wanting the abuse.
- You do not have to take it.
- If you believe your staying will help your partner, you are wrong. Your leaving may be the very thing that shocks him into realizing his behavior is against the laws of man and, more importantly, against the laws of God.
- You do have responsibility for your own life. With God's help you can make changes if you really want to.
- You are not alone. God is with you.
- If no one knows what is happening, there is nothing anyone can do. Stop hiding.
- Talk to someone. Ask for help. Others are ready and willing to help you.
- God is all-powerful. There is no problem he cannot solve.
- God has promised to be with his children always. Trust him!

Of course she was right! I knew all of this to be true. I had forgotten the larger narratives of Scripture as I had been so focused on the specific actions I should take as a wife, according to the Scriptures. The course of my life completely altered as I came out of denial and hiding and began to make decisions that would keep my children and me from any further harm. We were beloved! The message still makes me weep!

It's not what we do or what we have or what we have become that makes us loveable to God. Even my husband was God's beloved! The behavior however, was unacceptable and needed to be addressed.

WHAT IS ABUSE?

STATISTICS[1]

- On average, nearly 20 people per minute are physically abused by an intimate partner in the United States. During one year, this equates to more than 10 million women and men.
- 1 in 3 women and 1 in 4 men experience intimate partner physical violence, intimate partner sexual violence, and/or intimate partner stalking in their lifetime.
- 1 in 4 women and 1 in 7 men experience severe physical intimate partner violence in their lifetime.
- 1 in 7 women and 1 in 18 men have been stalked by an intimate partner during their lifetime to the point in which they felt very fearful or believed that they or someone close to them would be harmed or killed.
- On a typical day, there are more than 20,000 phone calls placed to domestic violence hotlines nationwide.

- The presence of a gun in a domestic violence situation increases the risk of homicide by 500%.
- Intimate partner violence accounts for 15% of all violent crime.
- Women between the ages of 18 to 24 are most commonly abused by an intimate partner.
- 19% of domestic violence involves a weapon.
- Domestic victimization is correlated with a higher rate of depression and suicidal behavior.
- Only 34% of people who are injured by intimate partners receive medical care for their injuries.
- Women who are sexually abused by intimate partners suffer severe and long-lasting physical and mental health problems, similar to those of other rape victims. They have higher rates of depression and anxiety than women who were either raped by a non-intimate partner or physically but not sexually abused by an intimate partner.

These statistics are appalling and should raise concern, but so many caught up in the cycle of domestic violence do not realize that they are being abused, or being abusive, as they are not aware of the definitions and dynamics and therefore have many misconceptions as to what domestic violence and abuse is. They often feel alone, as I did. Those interfacing with them are often in the dark as well. Definitions and education matter.

DEFINITIONS AND MISCONCEPTIONS

I define domestic violence as any word or deed that mars

the image of God in the other. In this way we become more cognizant of our own value and the value of all humankind. We also can become more attuned to our own propensities for harm, and become more accountable.

The Department of Justice defines domestic violence as,

> A pattern of abusive behavior in any relationship that is used by one partner to gain or maintain power and control over another intimate partner. Domestic violence can be physical, sexual, emotional, economic, or psychological actions or threats of actions that influence another person. This includes any behaviors that intimidate, manipulate, humiliate, isolate, frighten, terrorize, coerce, threaten, blame, hurt, injure, or wound someone.[2]

Domestic violence is often misunderstood. Most people picture the stereotypical abuser as a man beating a woman—a guy who severely hurts or kills his wife, and maybe even his children.

In reality, physical assault is only one feature of domestic violence. Most abuse happens verbally, emotionally, and psychologically: yelling, making scenes, threatening, giving orders, isolating family members, controlling economic resources, insisting on doing things only one way, constant criticism, and so on. It's really about coercive control: a situation where one person tries to control another through violence, fear (which can include intimidation and threats of violence), or by attacking another person's self-worth. In other words, it's easier to control another person if they are constantly afraid of being hurt, or if they are pushed to believe they are worthless. In this way, there is no need to physically assault or injure someone, because they are already compliant out of fear.

And contrary to popular belief, domestic violence is not an occasional expression of frustration or anger. It is not about a lack of submission, nor is it typically an isolated incident. Domestic violence, in all its forms, is a tool of coercion, and is a choice made by one person in a relationship to control another.

Many think that domestic violence happens only to certain kinds of people, but domestic violence can happen to anyone. It affects people from all classes, education levels, religions, and ethnic groups. It occurs in all types of relationships whether married, living together, or dating. The following is a short list of the types of abuse that can occur in families.

Physical Abuse: Hitting, slapping, shoving, grabbing, pinching, biting, hair pulling, etc. are types of physical abuse. This type of abuse also includes denying a partner medical care or forcing alcohol and/or drug use upon him or her.

Sexual Abuse: Coercing or attempting to coerce any sexual contact or behavior without consent. Sexual abuse includes, but is certainly not limited to, marital rape, attacks on sexual parts of the body, forcing sex after physical violence has occurred, or treating one in a sexually demeaning manner.

Emotional Abuse: Undermining an individual's sense of self-worth and/or self-esteem is abusive. This may include, but is not limited to constant criticism, diminishing one's abilities, name-calling, or damaging one's relationship with his or her children.

Economic Abuse: Making or attempting to make an individual financially dependent by maintaining total control over financial resources, withholding their access to money, or forbidding their attendance at school or employment.

Psychological Abuse: Elements of psychological abuse include—but are not limited to—causing fear by intimidation; threatening physical harm to self, partner, children, or partner's family or friends; destruction of pets and property; and forcing isolation from family, friends, or school and/or work.

The *effect* of domestic violence is also underestimated. Domestic violence not only hurts those who are abused, but also hurts family members and friends. Witnessing abuse impacts children; being abused violates the victim; and for those who abuse, trust and respect are jeopardized. According to the Department of Justice, children, who grow up being exposed to domestic violence are among those most adversely affected by it.[3] 1 in 15 children are exposed to intimate partner violence each year, and 90% of these children are eyewitnesses to this violence.[4]

> Children who are exposed to violence are at an increased risk for depression, anxiety, and attachment disorders. They often demonstrate more behavioral issues including aggression, non-compliance, delinquency, and symptoms related to posttraumatic stress disorder.[5]

Violence creates trauma. Trauma impacts us both mentally and physically, causing individuals to be easily overwhelmed, depressed, anxious, confused, or to shut down. Children may be affected differently based on their interpretation of the experience, how they have learned to survive and cope with the stress, the availability of support, and their ability to accept support and assistance from adults.

If a child learns that other people have the right to abuse them, or that women or others have no rights, it is fertile ground for Scripture to be twisted into false life-guiding beliefs. These beliefs then become barriers to seeing the gospel as a message of love, not one of exploitation, violence and death.

ADDRESSING SEVEN THEOLOGICAL DISTORTIONS ABOUT ABUSE

For churches, the statistics are equally sobering. Domestic violence is as prevalent in faith communities as outside of them.

Christians often turn to their faith community and spiritual leaders for help. The church community needs to be equipped to answer common questions from victims/survivors like:

- Where was God?
- Why did God allow this to happen to me?
- Is my sinfulness the cause of this?
- Do I need to forgive my abuser?

These questions reflect the victim's struggle to integrate beliefs with life experiences.

It is imperative for victims/survivors to understand that the Bible is a resource that shows God understands and provides for those who suffer from abuse. We must come to the scriptural text to consider its possible impact on victims/survivors for both good and evil. Some of the poor theology that is given to victims only serves as a barrier to safety and to accountability. Distorted Scripture enables abuse and prevents victims from seeking help.

Misquoting Scripture to cover abuse is harmful. God's Word never condones abuse. What follows are examples of twisted biblical messages that victims may hear.

I Am Suffering Because the Lord is Punishing Me.

Because there are examples in Scripture of God punishing those who sin, victims can easily conclude, "Because I am suffering, I must have sinned and am being punished by God."

The disciples also wondered if suffering was punishment for sin. In John 9, they met a blind man, and asked Jesus, "Who sinned, this man or his parents that he was born blind?" Jesus answered, "Neither this man nor his parents."

The blind man's suffering was not the result of God's response to sin; neither is a victim of domestic violence suffering as a result of their own sin. Sadly, they are suffering as a result of the abuser's sin.

God is not blind to the abuser's sin, even though it may feel as if God does not hear the victim's cries. Psalm 34:15–18, says,

> The eyes of the Lord are on the righteous and his ears are attentive to their cry. But the face of the Lord is against those who do evil to blot out their name from the earth. The righteous cry out, and the Lord hears them. He delivers them from all their troubles. The Lord is close to the broken hearted and saves those who are crushed in spirit.

YOUR NEEDS DON'T MATTER. YOU SHOULD BE PUTTING OTHERS FIRST.

Philippians 2:3–4 says, "Do nothing out of selfish ambition or vain conceit. Rather, in humility value others above yourselves, not looking to your own interests but each of you to the interests of the others."

While the New Testament writers exhort Christians to imitate

Christ's self-sacrifice in service to God, these Scriptures can be distorted to coerce someone to make sacrifices and concessions that are detrimental to physical, emotional, and spiritual health.

In Scripture we are also admonished to "love our neighbor as ourselves." This assumes that is it not selfish to take care of ourselves. It is not selfish or vain to desire adequate rest and food, safety, dignity, and respect.

You Need to Do A Better Job Submitting to Your Husband.

Ephesians 5:22 reads, "Wives, submit to your husbands as to the Lord."

Not only do some abusers use this verse to control their victim, but the victims themselves often believe that this verse requires a wife to accept her husband's abusive behavior. Using this logic, a Christian woman may conclude that to be a godly wife she should submit to whatever her husband says, does, or decides—including tolerating abuse.

But the subject of submission begins in Ephesians 5:21, "Submit to one another out of reverence for Christ." The verb "submit" is in verse 21, not in verse 22, implying that all of the instructions that follow are examples of how household members submit to one another.

The apostle Paul describes a godly relationship as one where both the wife and husband to submit to each other. This continues to be a very counter-cultural message, but this is what the Bible teaches; not domination, but mutual submission.

Domestic violence cannot exist within a relationship of mutual submission.

GOD HATES DIVORCE.

The concept that God hates divorce is well known to believers. These words seem to be clear and direct, but their interpretation is oversimplified.

In some translations, these three words, "I hate divorce" are part of a larger passage in Malachi 2:13–17. Yet these three can dominate people's thinking so that all the others go unheard. Furthermore, these three words are merely the beginning of a sentence.

The entire sentence in verse 16 in the *New American Bible*, Revised Edition reads, "'I hate divorce,' says the Lord God of Israel, 'and I hate a man's covering himself with violence as well as with his garment,' says the Lord Almighty." Clearly, God hates divorce and violence goes against God's design for marriage.

The text is directed toward Jewish men of that day who were abusing their wives but acting tenderly with them in public and then divorcing them to marry another.

Twice Malachi gives a strong directive (verses 15 and 16), "So guard yourself in your spirit, and do not break faith with the wife of your youth." Violence breaks faith. This passage is advocating for the welfare of the wife as well as God's desire for marriage.

When this teaching is misused, even if a woman contemplates escaping, she may stay out of fear of engendering God's hatred, or out of a misdirected reverence for God.

THE WIFE DOES NOT RULE OVER HER OWN BODY.

The first half of 1 Corinthians 7:4 is most frequently quoted, "The wife's body does not belong to her alone but also to her husband." Breaking the verse up in this way underscores the danger of stopping at the first half.

Some read this to say that if a wife does not rule her own body but her husband does, then it must be acceptable for him to rule over her physically in whatever way he wants. To be a godly wife then means to surrender to whatever he does or demands.

However, the verse in its entirety says, "The wife's body does not belong to her alone but also to her husband. In the same way, the husband's body does not belong to him alone but also his wife."

God desires open communication and mutual submission between husband and wife. This passage does not give license for domination or abuse.

FORGIVE AND FORGET.

Scripture teaches the importance of forgiving:
- "Forgive us our debts as we also have forgiven our debtors." (Matthew 6:12)
- "Bear with each other and forgive whatever grievances you may have against one another. Forgive as the Lord forgave you." (Colossians 3:13)
- "As far as the east is from the west, so far has he removed our transgressions from us." (Psalm 103:12)

Often when someone attempts to leave an abusive situation, the abuser, and sometimes others, will pressure the victim to forgive. It may be implied that to forgive is to forget the abuse and remain in the relationship. The lie told to victims is that to leave would be unforgiving and therefore sinful.

This is a shallow understanding of forgiveness. Forgiveness does not mean that one forgets the offense. Nor does forgiveness require reconciliation. Reconciliation may happen in time, if there is true repentance on the part of the abuser. But it is imperative that the penitent one demonstrate changed behavior over a long period of time. A victim's life could be endangered if she is reunited with the abuser before transformation is evident. Also, the victim needs time to work through multiple stages of forgiveness.

EVERYONE HAS A CROSS TO BEAR: GOD DOESN'T GIVE US MORE THAN WE CAN HANDLE.

If a victim of abuse is told that to suffer is to be like Jesus, she comes to believe abuse must simply be accepted as one's "cross to bear."

However, in the "take up your cross" passage, Jesus is not speaking to all forms of suffering, annoyances, and frustrations. He is specifically teaching on complete surrender of one's own agenda to God in order to follow God wholeheartedly, even to the point of death.

Jesus is our example of ultimate obedience to God, even to the point of suffering death. We too will suffer in our obedience to God's calling, but suffering for our faith is not the same as suffering abuse. The former is the cost of true discipleship; the latter is the result of one person's power and control over another, something that is never sanctioned by God's Word. Victims of abuse must never view their suffering abuse as God's will for them.

These seven messages are a few examples of how the church has contributed to violence through bad theology, while scores suffer in fear and silence.

How Should the Church Respond?

Appropriately addressing domestic violence in the church takes education, training, and spiritual reflection. In your own church, you can pursue education and training about the domestic violence to help you become a more effective resource and possibly even save a life.

While we can disagree on the roles of men and women, headship, and submission, we can all agree that God is close to the brokenhearted. As a church, our place is to be close to the brokenhearted as well. This includes all members of a family touched by violence, particularly children.

Safety is the most important work we can ever do as a faith community, as a community at large. As we strategize our responses, we must keep safety as our top priority. Wanting to be safe from beatings, threats, and fear is a well-established biblical precedent, not a sin. David fled from Saul, Paul fled Ephesus to escape a plot to murder him, Jesus' parents took him to Egypt to escape the murder of baby boys, and on multiple occasions he avoided situations that threatened his life. Church teaching that prioritizes safety and non-violent messages allows for someone being abused to hear that making a decision about safety first, is God-honoring. It may spur them on to make decisions that will protect them from further injuries, physically, emotionally, and spiritually, and propel them to much needed places of healing such as shelters and or counseling.

- Preach sermons that address domestic violence
- Believe the victim's story
- Support the choices of when or whether to call the police, leave etc

Scripture can be so helpful during these times. The larger narrative of God's love and provision in Scripture, and stories of those who have also lived through difficult times can bring much encouragement to the abused.

Build partnerships with local shelters and counselors specializing in domestic violence for education and referral purposes. Networking with advocates and counselors who specialize in abuse, can help with practical, emotional and spiritual needs. Letting a victim know that you care enough to make a careful referral can rebuild trust and hope. Being prepared in advance with resources and relationships allows for a more trusting referral.

Develop a policy to respond to domestic violence and make your congregation aware of it

Teach on healthy relationships from the pulpit, in marriage seminars, men's and women's ministries, children's ministries, camps and retreats, etc. Include the dynamics of these relationships centering around love: trust and support, shared responsibility, respect, fairness and negotiation, open communication, intimacy, honesty and responsibility, and physical affection.

Accountability for the abuser is key for lasting changes that make for safe intimate relationships. Those who perpetrate violence are committing sin at the expense of those who love and trust them. When domestic violence is confronted with intolerance, and the work is undertaken to promote the redemption of the abusing partner, there is reason to hope.

- Help the abuser to see themselves clearly and to learn the Christian disciplines of kindness, respect, love ,and the sacrifice of leadership
- Refer the abusive partner to appropriate community services and counseling that specialize in domestic violence. Staying in relationship is crucial during this time
- Help the abusive partner to accept that separation with intensive counseling and accountability may be required to allow for real change.
- Scripture may be a resource, reminding the abusive partner of the countless biblical stories that provide hope for change through repentance.

Caution: It is easy to collude with an abuser, so it is crucial that as a part of the accountability offered by the church for an abuser, there exists a partnership with counselors and community agencies that specialize in abuse and recovery. As domestic violence is a problem with the one who abuses, individual work and treatment programs are vital. Marriage counseling can have devastating consequences in these cases by re-victimizing the victim.

Along with safety and accountability, the church has the opportunity to be a safe place for the sinner to confess and repent from the sin of violence, and receive the gift of God's love and accountability for change. Following repentance, the church can even be a place of restoration for relationships and marriage. However, regardless of whether or not the marriage relationship is restored, grief and loss must be anticipated and worked through. Acknowledging that one is in an abusive marriage can cause as much pain for someone as leaving or ending the relationship. There may be multiple breakups because leaving is such a difficult choice. Shared histories, hopes, and dreams make the decisions to stay or break up harder for some than for others.

The church can allow for mourning and lament on the part of both the victim and perpetrator, as well as the extended family and community. Grief and loss is inherent to domestic violence. Historically when someone passes away, the church has provided meals, childcare, and cards to assist in the grieving process and to provide solace. These tangible acts of kindness and mercy are also immensely important for one who is separated because of domestic violence. They need a safe place with people who love and care for them and meet their basic needs.

There are many "woulda, coulda, shouldas" when it comes to domestic violence and abuse. Provide space for people to acknowledge the pain and suffering. Lament challenges the status quo of injustice and gives voice for change.

WHAT DOES THE LORD REQUIRE OF US? MICAH 6:8 SAYS…

Act justly—as Christians we have the responsibility to respond on behalf of the oppressed.

Love mercy—as Chrsitians we are uniquely poised to provide protection for the abused and hope for change for the abuser.

Walk humbly with God—as Christians we walk with him and care for his children as he has cared for us.

A good marriage is intimate, not just functional. Intimacy is based on equality and deepens with non-threatening behavior and respect, trust and support, honesty and accountability, responsible parenting, shared responsibility, economic partnership, negotiation, and fairness. Moving from a paradigm of power and control that creates fear to the power of love requires mutual respect and equality.

Perfect isn't the goal, and with every good marriage, come two flawed and imperfect people. These flaws, honored and cherished, are a part of our beautiful mess. The mess we bring each other, the mess we have the opportunity to live into, and the mess God loves to play in with us.

The mess, when we are safe, accountable and loving reconciles us to each other in a way that each person and family member has the opportunity to flourish in. This is the good news!

Questions for Discussion and Reflection

1. After reading this chapter, are there any false ideas about domestic violence that you have held?

2. What are the components of abuse, and why can it be more than physical?
3. This chapter identifies several false teachings on scripture and abuse. Are these familiar to you? What is actually true in answering these?

RECOMMENDED FOR FURTHER READING

No Place for Abuse: Biblical & Practical Resources to Counteract Domestic Violence by Catherine Clark Kroeger and Nancy Nason-Clark. Downers Grove, InterVarsity Press, 2010.

Domestic Violence: What Every Pastor Needs to Know (2nd Ed.) by Al Miles. Minneapolis: Fortress Press; 2011.

Strengthening Families and Ending Abuse: Churches and Their Leaders Look to the Future, Nancy Nason-Clark, Barbara Fisher-Townsend, and Victoria Fahlberg, editors. Eugene, Wipf and Stock, 2013.

The Courage Coach: A Practical, Friendly Guide on How to Heal from Abuse by Easter, Ashley., CreateSpace, 2017.

– 9 –
What about Divorce?

David Instone-Brewer

Divorce is often experienced as a double rejection: by a spouse and by the church. Many churches forbid divorce even on the grounds of abuse or abandonment, so that even an innocent victim can find themselves without support from fellow Christians when they need it most. This is due to a misunderstanding of Jesus' words on divorce.

At first glance, the New Testament teaching appears to be clear. Jesus said that the only valid ground for divorce is sexual immorality (normally understood as adultery), and that remarriage is equivalent to adultery (Matt. 5:31–32; 19:3–12; Mark 10:2–12; Luke 16:18). Paul seemingly contradicts Jesus, because he doesn't mention divorce for sexual immorality and instead he appears to allow divorce for abandonment by an unbeliever. Paradoxically, this is the only place where Paul says he is relying on Jesus' teaching (1 Cor. 7:10–16).

Virtually all churches conclude that the only valid ground for divorce is adultery. Most Protestants allow remarriage after a valid divorce, but the Catholic Church does not allow any remarriage unless the marriage can be shown to have been legally defective—the process of annulment. There is also a cautious acceptance that abandonment by an unbeliever may be an additional ground, though the definition of an "'unbeliever" is problematic. The usual conclusion is that Jesus has called believers to a higher lifestyle, though in the modern church, marriages fail as often as among non-believers.

Another area of debate is the definition of "sexual immorality" (*porneia* in Greek). In ancient literature, this word had a fairly wide meaning, including prostitution and adultery, but some modern interpreters have stretched it to include the use of pornography or even anything that hinders a marriage. The motive for these improbable interpretations is the clear impression that there is something missing from New Testament teaching. There is no apparent biblical remedy for spouses who are suffering neglect or abuse, even when it is dangerous. Even separating from one's partner is deemed to be forbidden by Paul (1 Cor. 7:10–11).

It appears that the New Testament teaching is illogical and impractical—Jesus and Paul contradict each other, and there is no pastoral solution for the problems of abuse or abandonment by a believer.

This apparent contradiction is due to a missing piece of information hidden in plain sight, among highly technical legally arcane rabbinic discussions about divorce. I stumbled across it while studying how the Pharisees interpreted the scriptures.

This discovery showed that divorce in Jesus' day was allowed for adultery, abandonment, and abuse, though some rabbis found a loophole that allowed no-fault divorces. Another surprise was that divorce was almost entirely egalitarian, until soon after Jesus' earthly ministry.

A CLUE IN ANCIENT JEWISH LAW

I didn't realize I'd found the missing piece to this puzzle until after my doctoral studies. In the ministry I faced many practical challenges which drove me to re-read the divorce passages. For some strange reason, they didn't look the same any more. Then I realized that I was reading them through the eyes of a first century rabbi.

Having spent three years reading everything the Pharisees had written, I understood their strange uses of Bible texts and their specialized terminology. I knew the specific ways in which they abbreviated their debates, and could expand their records like one adds water to a dehydrated meal. As I read the record of the Pharisees' debate with Jesus about divorce, the narrative took on new clarity and meaning.

I realized there were a couple of components missing to modern readers which were obvious to the first readers of the gospels. First there was the cultural context: everyone knew the normal way one got married and divorced, and Jesus didn't need to explain this to his audience. Second, there were specialized legal terms that were familiar to his audience. These terms were eventually forgotten and are no longer part of the context we have when we read these passages of Scripture.

Jesus wasn't the first person to debate the Pharisees' question about divorce. In records from later rabbis, we find that this debate started a generation before Jesus and continued for several decades after his death.

The debate regarding grounds for divorce started when Hillel, one of the founding Pharisees in the first century BC, discovered a loophole in Deuteronomy 24:1. This verse says you can get divorced for "immorality of a cause" (Hebrew: *ervat davar*). This strange phrase is usually turned around as if it says "a cause of immorality" and this is normally interpreted as adultery. That is how it was understood by Shammai, the founder of a rival school of Pharisees, and all modern Bibles follow this interpretation. But Hillel said the strangeness of this phrase implied something else.

Hillel's reasoning followed a normal pattern for rabbis at the time, even if it seems strange to us. He saw that Deuteronomy 24:1 makes perfect sense if you remove the word "cause." However, God is a perfect legislator, so this apparently superfluous word must refer to another valid "cause" for divorce. Now, the nature of this cause isn't stated, so Hillel concluded that this verse contains two grounds for divorce:

- 1) sexual immorality
- 2) any cause.[1]

In the records of the debate, the Hillelites claim that Deuteronomy 24:1 contained this second ground for divorce for "any-cause," and the Shammaites retort that the verse refers to "nothing except sexual immorality." These two phrases, "any cause" and "except sexual immorality," stood out when I re-read the gospel accounts:

> Pharisees came up to him and tested him by asking "Is it lawful to divorce one's wife for any cause?" He answered, "....whoever divorces his wife, except for sexual immorality, and marries another, commits adultery." (Matt. 19:3, 9)

When you employ the normal methods for unpacking abbreviated rabbinic debates and add these new insights about legal terminology being used at the time, these verses become:

> Pharisees came up to him and tested him by asking "Is it lawful to use the any-cause divorce [based on Deut. 24:1]?" He answered, "... whoever divorces [on the basis of this verse for anything] except sexual immorality, and marries another, commits adultery." (Matt. 19:3, 9)

The adulterous nature of this remarriage is now obvious. Jesus rejected this ground for divorce, so anyone who had remarried after using the "any cause" divorce was actually still married to their first partner!

THE POPULAR NEW ANY-CAUSE DIVORCE

These two phrases ("for any cause" and "except for sexual immorality"), are present only in Matthew and are missing in Mark's otherwise similar account. This puzzled me, until I realised the question asked in Mark is, strictly speaking, meaningless. If the intention was to only ask: "Is it lawful for a man to divorce his wife?" (Mark 10:2) Jesus could have answered: "Of course it is lawful, because it is written in the law—dummy!" Matthew shows us the Pharisees were asking a more complex question in an abbreviated form.

We ask similarly meaningless questions but they don't sound stupid. For example, "Is it lawful for a 16-year old to drink?" If you answer "No," you have done one of two things: You have either condemned all teenagers to die of thirst, or you have mentally added the words "alcoholic beverages" to the question. First century Jews did the same thing when they read Mark's gospel. The Pharisees' question was very familiar to them, so they mentally added the words "... for any-cause."

By the time Matthew was written, the debate was already starting to fade from peoples' memory, so he helpfully added the implied words as a reminder. However, by the second century even this reminder was not enough, because the early church leaders misunderstood it. And by the third century even some rabbis had forgotten the meaning of this language.[2] This legal terminology was forgotten because the any-cause divorce became the normal and sole form of divorce, so no-one debated it any more. But during the time of Jesus, it was still a subject of active and popular discussion.

When a Jewish couple faced divorce, the whole family suddenly had to become familiar with legal language, just as we have to understand phrases like *prenuptial agreement*. They had to pick three lawyers to hear their case, so should they pick a Hillelite or a Shammaite? If you wanted an any-cause divorce—and most people did—you needed to know that Hillelites allowed it and Shammaites didn't. An any-cause divorce could be granted for any tiny thing including a new wrinkle or burnt soup—these were actual examples suggested by lawyers![3] Also, it would be granted automatically. There was no need for a trial where your neighbors listened to all your accusations and faults, so this interpretation of the grounds for divorce quickly become very popular.

Though this type of divorce could only be brought by a man (because of the context of Deut. 24:1), women preferred it because it guaranteed the woman would get financial support due to her. When couples married, the man promised his wife a minimum of 200 *zuz* (about a year's basic wage) if he died or divorced her. However, she lost this if the divorce was her fault—for example if she committed adultery but there weren't two witnesses to enable the death penalty. However, with an any-cause divorce, she knew that she would get the full settlement because there was no court case to apportion guilt.

The any-cause divorce quickly became the most popular form of divorce. Even Joseph planned to use it when ending his betrothal to Mary. He could have easily charged her with adultery, but "being a just man and unwilling to put her to shame, he resolved to divorce her quietly" (Matt. 1:19). The any-cause divorce, which involved no court hearing, must have been what he had in mind. By the end of the century we stop hearing about grounds for divorce because the only form of divorce in use was the any-cause divorce.

TRADITIONAL BIBLICAL DIVORCES

In Jesus' day one could still get divorced on biblical grounds, based on the words of Exodus 21:10–11.

> If he marries another woman, he must not deprive the first one of her food, clothing and marital rights. If he does not provide her with these three things, she is to go free, without any payment of money.

These verses were written or referred to in all the marriage certificates that have survived from the first two centuries. Karaite Jews, who rejected Pharisaic innovations such as the any-cause divorce, continued to record them in their marriage certificates until the 10th century. But mainstream Judaism adopted any-cause as their only means for divorce by the end of the first century, so the biblical grounds in Exodus were soon forgotten. Unfortunately they were forgotten by the church too, even though Christian marriage vows are based on them.

At first glance, Exodus 21:10–11 has nothing to do with

marriage or divorce—they are regulations about slavery. The law says that if you marry a slave girl but fail to supply her with food, clothing and love, then she can go free. However, the rabbis recognized that the laws of Moses usually defined the most minor circumstance so that the law would automatically apply to more serious situations. For example, when the law said you shouldn't deprive an ox from the benefits of his labor (i.e. eating some grain while treading it—see Deut. 25:4), this law also applied to anyone more important than an ox, such your human employees. That's why Paul cited this law with regard to paying church workers (1 Cor. 9:9; 1 Tim. 5:18). Similarly, when Exodus made laws about the rights of female slaves, these rights applied automatically to non-slaves, both male and female.

This law meant that both men and women could gain a divorce in Jesus' day if they could show that they suffered neglect with regard to food, clothing, or love. This wasn't a matter of debate; as far as we know, all Jewish groups in the early first century agreed on this point. Even the Hillelites and Shammaites both accepted this interpretation, though they normally disagreed with each other on reflex, like Republicans and Democrats. After all, God himself spoke about his marriage to Israel in these terms. When Ezekiel described the reasons why God divorced Israel, he describes the food, clothing, and love that God provided, and how Israel had adulterously shared that food, clothing, and love with the idols (Ezek. 16:10–19).

The Pharisees took these grounds for divorce so seriously that they recorded the minimum food and clothing, and how long one had to be deprived of love, for these to qualify as neglect. Neglect occurred if the husband didn't provide food and cloth (or money) or the wife didn't cook and sew.[4] The rabbinic lawyers said that neglect of love-making depended on your occupation. A camel-riding trader could be away for a month but an ass-driver could only excuse himself for a week. All other workers had to do their duty twice a week, and the unemployed every day! However, they made a concession for themselves: scholars could take a month off.[5]

The significance of all these details is that the Pharisees who were questioning Jesus clearly assumed, like everyone else, that both a woman and a man could demand a divorce for neglect. In fact, half of all the surviving divorce certificates from the first two centuries record divorces brought by women. (I'd better admit that this is a misleading statement, because only two divorce certificates have survived from that period; but one of them does record a woman divorcing her husband.[6])

One slight problem was that only the man could actually write the divorce certificate and he had to do this willingly. The later rabbis recorded the solution to this: they beat him with rods until he was willing (Mishnah Arakin 5.6).

Abuse was also a ground for divorce, because of the principle that the law defines the least important circumstance in order to include everything more serious. Modern law codes work in the same way, so "battery" is often defined as any touch which is inappropriate, and this automatically includes anything worse. In the same way, ancient Jewish law forbade neglect, and this automatically included anything worse such as abuse. Abandonment was also included because even if they arranged for food and clothing to be delivered, an absent spouse was neglecting to share their love.

So why doesn't the New Testament refer to divorce for abandonment and abuse when it was a fundamental right of all Jewish men and women? Jesus and Paul didn't have to teach these grounds for divorce, because everyone already accepted them. Even the Greek-Roman world used similar terms in their marriage contracts. In the same way the New Testament doesn't have to state that rape is wrong, because everyone already knew that. So we shouldn't expect a statement about these grounds for divorce, unless the New Testament writers wanted to specifically deny that such divorces were wrong. However, now that we know what to look for, we can actually find allusions to these grounds for divorce.

JESUS' TEACHING

Before looking for abuse and abandonment, we need to understand what Jesus actually said about adultery. We can now see that when he was asked what he thought about "divorce for any cause" this didn't mean "Do you agree with any kind of divorce at all?" but rather, "Do you agree with the new any-cause divorce?" At first, Jesus didn't answer the question, because he was more interested in talking about marriage than divorce.

He criticized the practice of polygamy which was common at the time in Palestine. He quoted Genesis 2:24 with an additional word: "Therefore a man shall leave his father and his mother and hold fast to his wife, and the **two** shall become one flesh" (Matt. 19:5). We are now so used to seeing the verse cited in this way that we don't notice that the word "two" has been added for emphasis. Jesus was saying that a marriage involves two and only two people. In this he was agreeing with the Jews of the Dead Sea Scrolls who also emphasizsed this. He also criticised those Pharisees who said that a man whose wife commits adultery *must* divorce her. They said "Moses commanded one to give a certificate of divorce." Jesus corrected them: "Moses *allowed* you to divorce your wives." On this point he agreed with many Hillelites.

Jesus also emphasized forgiveness rather than divorce. He said that divorce should only occur when there is "hard-heartedness" (Greek *sklerokardia*, Matt. 19:8). This word occurs nowhere in Greek literature, because it was invented by Greek translators of the Old Testament. Because the word occurs only twice, and only one of those relates to divorce, Jesus is clearly alluding to a specific Bible verse—Jeremiah 3:3. Jeremiah said that God divorced Israel because she was sinning hard-heartedly—i.e. stubbornly and persistently. Israel's divorce was enacted when she was sent into exile for seventy years. Jeremiah described this as one year for every seven years that Israel had rebelled (2 Chron. 36:21). In other words, God had forgiven Israel seven times seventy times before he decided that divorce was the only remedy.

Some think that Jesus also criticized the divorce law of Moses, saying that this was given only "because of your hardness of heart" (Matt. 19:8)—as if the Jews had harder hearts so, unlike Christians, they needed provision for divorce. However, I think it more likely that Jesus was referring to the pervasive condition of humans, because we are all capable of stubborn sinfulness. God reluctantly allows victims to divorce unfaithful, abusive, and abandoning partners, because we are all capable of sinning hardheartedly. Jesus did not supplant the moral law of the Old Testament. In fact he criticized those who rejected the tiniest part of it (Matt. 5:17). He came to fulfill the ceremonial law and write the moral law on our hearts.

When eventually the Pharisees dragged him back to talking about the any-cause divorce, Jesus rejected it totally. He clearly agreed with the Shammaite position, and even cited their slogan approvingly. The Shammaites said one couldn't derive the any-cause divorce from the phrase "cause of sexual immorality" because this was a single phrase; they said it referred to "nothing except sexual immorality." Siding with the Shammaites in this case didn't make Jesus into a Shammaite. As we saw above, he had just sided with the Jews of the Dead Sea Scrolls community who were against polygamy, and with some Hillelites who were against compulsory divorce for adultery. Jesus was entirely independent.

Jesus regarded the any-cause divorce as totally invalid. To emphasise this he said: "If you remarry after an any-cause divorce you are committing adultery"—because the original marriage had not ended. Since virtually all divorces at that time were based on any-cause, this could be simplified as: "Anyone who remarries is committing adultery" (Mark 10:11; Luke 16:18). The Gospels used this attention-grabbing rhetoric as a summary statement which (like most summaries) is confusing and misleading without understanding the background details.

Is this interpretation correct? An ancient Jewish reader may understand it like this, but we find it easier to understand it differently. A modern reader thinks Jesus is being asked if divorce is ever right, and he answers: only in the case of adultery. So which meaning is correct? We need enough humility to realize that the gospel writers were communicating primarily to readers in their days. We have to read over their shoulders, so we must translate not just the words, but seek to understand the meaning of the terminology at the time it was written.

JESUS ON ABUSE AND ABANDONMENT

We now know how Jesus' audience would have understood him. He was denying the validity of the newly invented any-cause divorce. But which grounds for divorce did Jesus regard as valid? Jesus wasn't asked that, and he doesn't tell us. He did mention the ground of adultery ,but only in order to answer the question about the any-cause divorce. So why didn't Jesus tell us which grounds he agreed with, and the rights of people who suffer abandonment or abuse?

Divorce is just one of a multitude of things that Jesus doesn't tell us, because he doesn't have to. Jesus didn't normally tell people what they already knew—or at least, the gospel writers didn't spend precious papyrus repeating it for us. Jesus doesn't tell us the difference between murder and manslaughter, or tell us rules about charging interest, or using fair weights, or how to distinguish between a rape and consensual sex. He doesn't have to teach about any of these things because they were already covered in God's law, which he said he supported. He claimed to say the same as his Father, so it would sound strange if he contradicted the Old Testament law.

All the Jews listening to Jesus knew that biblical grounds for divorce included the neglect of food, clothing, and love, which automatically implied the more serious offenses of abandonment and abuse. These grounds were recorded in their marriage certificates and were taught by all branches of Judaism at the time. If Jesus had wanted to deny them, he would have had to teach strongly against them. To affirm them, he could simply do the same as he did on the subject of rape: he merely had to remain silent.

Paul on Remarriage

Paul did not remain silent on the matters of neglect and abandonment because although Greeks and Romans had remarkably similar views about neglect within marriage, non-Jewish converts did not know God's law as well as Jews. However, he was remarkably silent about remarriage. This was very common in the Roman world due to their extremely easy no-fault divorce. Roman divorce-by-separation required no statement of grounds or fault; you simply had to tell your spouse to pack and leave or (if they owned the house) you just walked out. This was even easier than the Jewish any-cause divorce that Jesus rejected. It resulted in instant divorce, without any paperwork or court appearance, and you didn't even need the consent of your spouse.

A woman in the church at Corinth wanted to use this Roman divorce-by-separation. Paul told her to remain with her husband, and if she had already separated she should ask to be reconciled (1 Cor. 7:10–11). She couldn't simply return, because in Jewish law the victim always has the right to decide what will happen. She had walked out, so her husband now had the right to either regard this abandonment as a ground for divorce, or he could forgive her and be reconciled. The Jewish principle was that the victim always decides—and Paul appears to regard this as a biblical principle.

But what if she weren't a Christian? In that case she wouldn't listen to Paul, and her husband would remain abandoned. So Paul told people in those circumstances that they were "no longer bound" (1 Cor. 7:15). He can't mean they aren't bound by the marriage, because in Roman law their marriage is already finished. So presumably he means that are properly divorced and free to remarry.

Actually, in Roman law, they were obliged to remarry. In 18 BC a Roman law mandated that all divorcees must remarry within 12 months, because Augustus wanted to increase the number of legitimate Roman citizens. So if Paul was against remarriage he would have to state this very clearly, because he would be asking believers in Roman towns to risk prosecution. But all that Paul mentions on the subject of remarriage is found in a couple of ambiguous verses which say that marriage is ended by death (1 Cor. 7:39; Rom. 7:2–3). They are ambiguous because they don't say that marriage only ends by means of death; it is just that they don't mention divorce as another possible way to end a marriage. And that is to be expected, because the context in both cases concerns death—one is addressed to widows, and the other is a metaphor about death with Christ—so there's no reason to mention divorce in either. Paul remained silent—he did not forbid remarriage— so we have to assume remarriage was permitted, as in Old Testament law.

CHRISTIAN MARRIAGE VOWS

Modern marriage vows are based on Exodus 21:10–11, which Paul alludes to when he speaks about what marriage entails. He tells those who wish to abstain from sexual relations that they should do this only for a short period, because of their duty to their spouse (1 Cor. 7:3–5). When the rabbis discussed this same issue, they did it in a much more legalistic way. Paul also expected his readers to know about the requirements to supply food and clothing because he talks about the concerns for material support within marriage (1 Cor. 7:32—34). So although Paul doesn't spell it out, he clearly expected his readers to follow the laws about supplying food, clothing, and love to their spouse. And if they knew this, they would also know that these were the standard grounds for divorce.

The wording for our modern vows was influenced by the version of them in Ephesians which records the wedding vows of Jesus for his church: he promised to love her, nourish her and cherish her (Eph. 5:25–29). The words "nourish" and "cherish" translate Greek words for feeding and clothing children. In other words, these are ways of expressing the three-fold vows to provide food, clothing, and conjugal love. This same transition from legal terminology to nicer-sounding language is found in later Jewish and Christian marriages which refer to "love, honor, and keep." And the fourth ground for divorce based on Deuteronomy 24:1 was also included: "be faithful."

In the Jewish world of Jesus, breaking any of these marriage vows could trigger a divorce. The aggrieved partner could bring evidence to a rabbinic court, or they could decide to forgive instead. Jesus emphasized forgiveness. Just because a partner has done wrong did not mean that the other party must divorce them. Jesus wanted our first reaction to be forgiveness and said broken vows should only lead to divorce if there was "hardness of heart." By using this unusual word, Jesus reminded them of Jeremiah who said that Israel had sinned so persistently and unrepentantly (i.e. hardheartedly) that God had reluctantly divorced her.

It is remarkable that the Bible portrays God himself as a reluctant divorcee who seeks remarriage. Jeremiah questions whether God can remarry Israel because the law forbids remarrying someone you have divorced (Jer. 3:1, 6–8; Deut. 24:1–4). But the prophets said there would be a New Covenant in which the two former nations of Israel and Judah would be united as new nation—i.e. a brand new bride—who was later revealed to include the church (Jer. 31:31–34; Ezek. 37:15–28; Rev. 21:9–14).

Many churches reject people who are divorced, implicitly labelling them as having committed an unforgivable sin. Divorcees or those who remarry are often barred from communion and from holding leadership positions. But being a divorcee or remarried cannot be regarded as sinful if God can be described in these terms. God's divorce was based on all four biblical grounds (as we saw above): Israel was unfaithful by committing adultery with the idols and Ezekiel says that she gave them the food, clothing, and love that was due to God.

Malachi recorded God's anger against the non-biblical divorces of wives who had done nothing wrong (Mal. 2:13–16). When this practice become institutionalized in Hillel's new any-cause divorce, Jesus was equally critical. Today's no-fault divorce does essentially the same thing, though now it can be employed by both men and women to divorce an innocent partner against their will.

Jesus supported marriage by decrying the no-fault divorce of his day, but he did not intend us to abandon the biblical grounds for divorce. Instead, he wanted to allow divorce only on these grounds. He denied the any-cause divorce because it was the opposite of these biblical grounds by allowing divorce without the grounds of adultery, abuse, or abandonment or even the lesser fault of neglect.

I would love to see churches reaffirm these biblical grounds for divorce, and help build strong marriages while they work to reduce divorce for inconsequential reasons. We should also stop all discrimination against those who are divorced, especially when they are innocent victims.

However, change is difficult for churches whose doctrine is enshrined in a long-held misunderstanding of Jesus' teaching. Lack of awareness of the ancient legal formulas used in the gospels has led us all into illogical and impractical doctrines that won't be easy to correct. Even if a church accepts this new understanding, they will need humility and patience to change practices established by tradition. We all know that the larger the ship, the longer it takes to turn, and some of our churches have rudders that are stiff with centuries of rust. They can only be moved by prayer and the oil of the Holy Spirit.

SUMMARY OF KEY POINTS

- Jesus was asked not about divorce in general but about the new 'any-cause' divorce that was effectively a no-fault divorce.
- Jesus rejected it, saying that the verse it was based on

(Deut. 24:1) referred to nothing but sexual indecency.

- This new divorce soon supplanted biblical divorces for adultery, abuse and abandonment (which were based on Deut. 24:1 & Ex. 21:10-11).
- Jesus didn't need to affirm these biblical grounds for divorce, because everyone at that time accepted them.
- Paul didn't affirm them either, but his teaching in 1 Corinthians 7 implies that he agreed with them.
- Paul rejected the Roman no-fault divorce-by-separation just as Jesus rejected the Jewish no-fault divorce.
- Traditional Christian wedding vows are based on the biblical grounds for divorce.

QUESTIONS FOR DISCUSSION AND REFLECTION

1. "Adultery, Abuse, and Abandonment" is an easy-to-understand summary, but is it accurate? Which of the following would you want to include: neglect, emotional battery, distain, hatred, or others?
2. If the church for centuries has misunderstood phrases like "divorce for any cause," does this mean we can't be sure what the Bible says? Do you think there are other areas where our understanding might prove to be wrong?
3. Do you know of individuals that have felt rejected by the church? What changes would you make to help them feel more welcome?
4. Think of when you've heard vows made at weddings, or when you made vows yourself. Do you think those making the vows realize the seriousness of what they

are promising? What would you ask them to consider before making those vows?

RECOMMENDED FOR FURTHER READING

Divorce and Remarriage in the Church: Biblical Solutions for Pastoral Realities by David Instone-Brewer. Carlisle, Cumbria: Paternoster Press 2003 & Downers Grove: InterVarsity Press, USA 2007. This explains in more detail the basis and outworking of what this chapter says.

Remarriage After Divorce in Today's Church: 3 Views by Paul E. Engle, Mark L. Strauss, Gordon John Wenham, William A. Heth, and Craig Keener. Grand Rapids, Zondervan, 2006. This presents the main alternative ways of understanding these difficult texts.

Divorce and Remarriage: Biblical Principles and Pastoral Practice by Andrew Cornes. London, Hodder & Stoughton, 1993. This is the best biblical and pastoral presentation of the no-divorce interpretation.

www.DivorceRemarriage.com
Lots of resources including the wonderful PlayMobile presentations and videos.

Appendix

Inter-Testamental Background Regarding Jewish and Early Christian Views about Women

Manfred T. Brauch

During the Intertestamental period, between the completion of the Hebrew Bible (our Old Testament) and the New Testament, dating from about 300 BC to 100 AD, a decisively negative view of women developed within Judaism. Jewish teachers, some of whose writings during this period are preserved in the Apocrypha and Pseudepigrapha, as well as in the Talmud, taught that women were the weaker sex, less than men, and chiefly responsible for the fall. These beliefs were based primarily on interpretations of passages in Genesis, and became the foundation for such ideas as women's servant status and the unreliability of their testimony. This appendix highlights the teachings of several Jewish writers from this period, as well as the writings of early Christian leaders and scholars who subscribed to similar patriarchal views.

In a passage about particularly serious forms of evil (Sirach 25:13-23), we read: "Any wound, only not a heart-wound! Any wickedness, only not the wickedness of a woman!" (25:13). This assessment is grounded in the observation that "from a woman, sin did originate, and because of her we all must die." (25:24). Therefore, "if she does not do what you ask of her, cut her off from your flesh" (25:26 – meaning, "If she does not obey you, divorce her.") These sentiments are further expressed in 42:14, where "the wickedness of a man" is judged as "better... than the goodness of a woman."[1]

In a legendary conversation between Eve and Adam after the fall (in the Books of Adam and Eve), she addresses Adam as "my Lord" throughout, and confesses that "I have brought trouble and anguish upon you" (V. 3). In another passage, she asks Adam whether he would slay her, for perhaps then "the Lord will bring you into paradise, for on my account you have been driven from there." The interpretation of Genesis 3:16 as a divine command is clearly expressed in a passage where the archangel Joel, speaking on behalf of God, castigates Adam for listening to a suggestion by Eve: "I did not create your wife to command you, but to obey ..."[2]

A rabbinic interpretation of Genesis 18:15 (where Sarah is caught in a lie) concluded that women were by nature deceptive, and therefore their testimony could not be trusted. To teach Torah (the Jewish Law) to a woman was tantamount to teaching her promiscuity. Indeed, it was considered better to burn up the Torah, rather than to deliver it into the hands of women. For men to talk much with women was considered a source of evil that would ultimately lead to severe divine judgment.[3]

The first-century Jewish philosopher-theologian, Philo of Alexandria, in his reflections on Genesis 2:21, asks why the woman, unlike the man (and the animals!) was not formed from the earth. His answer is that, "First, because woman is not equal in honor with man. Second, because she is not equal in age, but younger. Third [God] wishes that man should take care of woman as a very necessary part of him, but woman, in turn, should serve him as a whole." (in Philo's commentary Genesis, Book I, 17). In reference to Genesis 3:1 he asks: "Why does the serpent speak to the woman and not to the man?" His answer is: "A woman is more accustomed to be deceived than men....Because of softness, she easily gives way and is taken in by plausible falsehoods which resemble the truth." (Genesis, Book I, 33).[4]

His younger contemporary, the Jewish historian Josephus, wrote: "From women let no evidence be acceptable because of the levity and temerity of their sex, neither let slaves bear witness because of the baseness of their soul...for they will not attest the truth."[5] These attitudes are comprehensively expressed in one of the "Eighteen Benedictions" prayed regularly by Jewish men, in which God is praised for not having created them either slaves, or gentiles, or women.[6]

Jewish practice in the first century reflects the impact of these perspectives. In keeping with the negative view of their reliability and trustworthiness, women's testimony was not acceptable in a court of law. They were restricted from studying Torah. In Synagogue worship, they were segregated behind a curtain and not permitted to participate actively and vocally in the worship liturgy. The main sanctuary of the temple was reserved for Jewish men, while women were relegated to a lower level outside the main sanctuary, called "the court of women."[7]

Not all voices within the Jewish tradition joined this negative chorus regarding the value and status of women. In some Jewish texts, the first man—not the woman—is held responsible for the entrance of sin and death into the world. In reflecting on the origin of sin and evil, the author of the apocryphal book, 4 Ezra, states that God gave Adam but one command to observe, "but he transgressed it" (4 Ezra 3:7). He goes on to say, "For the first Adam, clothing himself with the evil heart, transgressed and was overcome (4 Ezra 3:21; cf., 7:11–12). Then there is the lament in 4 Ezra 7:18, "O Adam, what have you done! For though it was you who sinned, the fall was not yours alone, but ours also who are your descendants!"[8] Paul's use of "Adam" (Rom. 5:14; 1 Cor. 15:22) and "one man" or "a human being" (Rom. 5:12; 1 Cor. 15:21) as the antithesis to "Christ" (Rom. 5:14; 1 Cor. 15:22; cf. 15:45–49) is in line with these exceptions to the overwhelming insistence in Jewish thought on Eve's culpability. Unfortunately, these alternative voices were largely muted in the louder chorus and did not impact the development of Christian views in the first centuries in any significant way. To the contrary, the writings of early church leaders during the first few centuries show ample evidence that the negative view about women in Judaism, which relegated them to subservient status in relation to men, prevailed.

The commentaries by early church fathers on Genesis 1–3 clearly reflect traditional Jewish interpretations of these texts.

Ephrem the Syrian (AD 306–373) seems to echo the view expressed in The Books of Adam and Eve (see above), when he states: "She [Eve] hastened to eat before her husband... that she might become the one to give command to that one by whom she was to be commanded..." Irenaeus (AD 135–202) wrote: "As the human race was subjected to death through the act of a virgin, so was it saved by a virgin; thus the disobedience of the one virgin was precisely balanced by the obedience of another." (Several other church fathers contended that Adam and Eve had no sexual relations before the fall. Thus Eve was considered a virgin before she was tempted.)[9] Commenting on Genesis 2:20, Augustine (AD 354–430) states that "he [Adam] rules and she [Eve] obeys. He is ruled by wisdom; she, by the man."[10]

In their reflections on New Testament passages regarding the relationship between husbands and wives, the early church fathers revealed their indebtedness to the thinking of their Jewish forbears. For example, Ambrose of Milan (AD 333–397) states that "she who was made as a helper needs the protection of the stronger....Yet, while he believed he would have the assistance of his wife, he fell because of her."[11] In reference to Genesis 2:23, Ambrosiaster (4th century AD) says that "although man and woman are of the same substance, the man has relational priority....He is greater than she is by cause and order, but not by substance."[12] Likewise, Theodoret of Cyr (AD 393–466) holds that "Man has first place because of the order of creation." In speaking of the significance of this primacy of man, he states that "the woman was created to serve [man], not the other way around."[13]

Many early Christian teachers read New Testament texts about women (e.g., 1 Cor.; Eph. 5; 1 Tim. 2) also through the lens of the Jewish interpretive tradition of the creation and fall narratives and were influenced in their interpretation of these texts by prevailing cultural norms. However, like in Judaism, there were also contrary voices among the Greek Fathers of the church, who heard those texts speak to them differently.

What these brief and representative examples reveal about both Jewish and early Christian interpretations and understandings of biblical texts is the truth expressed by Paul in 2 Corinthians 4:7, that we hold God's revelation "in our earthen vessels." This means that at times we get it wrong, we misunderstand biblical text. And at times we human beings are so captive to prevailing cultural practices and norms that we hear those voices more clearly than the authentic biblical voice.

Telford Work, in his *Living and Active: Scripture in the Economy of Salvation*, makes this powerful and insightful observation:

> "The history of the earthly Jesus is the story of the eternal Word brought into the fallen world and put at its mercy (Mark 14:41). In the same way, God's investment in the words of Scripture means that in the short term, in their own journey into the world, the divine words are subject to a similar submission

to and separation from their heavenly speaker, and a similar surrender to sinful speakers and hearers... In delivering [the Bible] to the world, God makes his words vulnerable, for a time, to abuse."

It is my conviction that the hierarchical interpretation of biblical texts about the relationship between men and women, and specifically between husbands and wives, is such an instance of abuse.

End Notes

Chapter 1 Genesis: A Very Good Place to Start

1. See Mildred Pagelow, in *Woman-Battering: Victims and Their Experiences* (Thousand Oaks, CA: Sage Publications, 1981), develops a theoretical framework for understanding wife battering, in which she identifies "traditional ideology" regarding male-female relationships as a major contributor to the abuse of women. See also Robert G. Clouse and Bonidell Clouse, eds., *Women in Ministry. Four Views* (Downers Grove, IL: InterVarsity Press, 1989), pp. 4-21. The historian R. Clouse surveys the various historical, cultural and ecclesiastical factors and developments in this matter of the role of women in the church. He concludes that "this is one of the most pressing problems facing believers in the closing years of the 20th century." See also James and Phyllis Alsdurf, *Battered Into Submission: The Tragedy of Wife Abuse in the Christian Home* (Downers Grove, IL: InterVarsity Press, 1998).

2. Eugene Peterson, in *The Message*, translates the Hebrew of Genesis 1:26 with "Let us make human beings in our image," thereby recognizing the generic meaning of *adam* in this text.

3. Ray S. Anderson and Dennis B. Guernsey, in *On Being Family: A Social Theology of the Family* (Grand Rapids, MI: Eerdmans, 1985), pp. 17-18, speak of this as "co-humanity": "Theological anthropology, drawing upon biblical teaching [shows that] the solitary person cannot share fully in the complete human existence. . . . According to the creation account in Genesis 2, co-humanity is the original and therefore quintessential aspect of personal and individual human existence." See also Mary S. VanLeuwen, *Gender and Grace: Love, Gender and Parenting in a Changing World* (Downers Grove, IL: InterVarsity Press, 1990), pp. 38-41, who contends that an important dimension of the image of God is our sociability: ". . . we are so

unshakably created for community that we cannot even develop as full persons unless we grow up in nurturing contact with others," including especially "fellowship with the opposite sex."

4. In the ancient Near East, it was common for a conquering monarch to leave a statue, an "image" of himself in the conquered territory, as a visible reminder of his continuing sovereignty over it. In creation, God conquers chaos, creates order, and places the human creation within it as God's image, to exercise responsible dominion within and over creation.

5. Mary Stewart Van Leuwen, *Gender and Grace* (Downers Grove, Ill: InterVarsity Press, 1990), p. 42.

6. Cited in Andrew Louth, ed., *Genesis 1-11. Ancient Christian Commentary on Scripture, Old Testament I* (Downers Grove, IL: InterVarsity Press, 2001), p. 28.

7. Even in English usage, the word "helper" has a range of possible meanings. Besides the meaning "assistant" or "servant" (as in "hired help"), the word can also refer to someone in a superior position (as when someone throws a life-line to a drowning person), or in a position of authority (such as a professor, who was of great help in my dissertation research).

8. Some early church fathers interpreted the woman's relationship to the man in that way. Ephrem the Syrian wrote that the woman as man's helper meant that she would "help the man" with the various tasks in agriculture and animal husbandry. Augustine likewise understands the woman as man's helper in the sense of the relationship between ruler (the man) and ruled (the woman). Ambrose contends that the woman is called "helper" in the sense of "the generation of the human family—a really good helper" and then gives an analogy from his own time: "We see people in high and important offices often enlist the help of people who are below them in rank and esteem." See Andrew Louth, ed. *Genesis 1-11. Ancient Christian Commentary on Scripture. Old Testament I* (Downers Grove, IL: InterVarsity Press, 2001), pp. 68-69.

9. Isa 30:5; Eze 12:14; Da 11:34

10. E.g., Ex 18:4; Dt 33:7, 26, 29; 1Sa 7:12; Ps(s) 33:20; 46:1; 70:5; 115:9, 10, 11; 121:1, 2).

11. See Samuel Terrien, *Til the Heart Sings: A Biblical Theology of Manhood and Womanhood* (Philadelphia, PA: Fortress Press, 1985), pp 9-10, who writes: "The ancient mentality, especially the Hebraic, considered aloneness as the negation of authentic living, for true life is not

individual but corporate and social. The Hebrew word translated 'alone' (Ge 2:18) carries an overtone of separation and even of alienation. Human beings live only insofar as they are related in their environment to partners with whom they share mutuality and complementariness. Animals do not fulfill the requirements of true partnership." See also G. Ernest Wright, *The Old Testament Against its Environment* (London: SCM Press, 1951).

12. The first-century Jewish philosopher Philo of Alexandria, who is generally not an advocate of women's equality, understands the *ezer kenegdo* of Ge 2:18 and 20 to "refer to partnership . . . with those who bring mutual benefit . . . To everyone of those who come together in the partnership of love, the saying of Pythagoras can be applied, that 'a lover is indeed another self.'" See *Questions and Answers on Genesis, I.17.* Loeb Classical Library (Cambridge: Harvard University Press, 1937).

13. Andrew Louth, ed., *Ancient Christian Commentary on Scripture: Old Testament* (Downers Grove, IL: IVP Academic), 1:92.

14. Helmut Thielicke, *How the World Began: Man in the First Chapters of the Bible* (Philadelphia, PA: Muelenberg Press, 1961), argues persuasively that we miss the great theological insights of these narratives if we read them as literalistic-historical accounts rather than as theological faith affirmations in the form of poetry and narrative. See also G. E. Wright, *Studies in Biblical Theology,* No. 2 (London: SCM Press, 1957), shows that the OT's central theological affirmations must be understood as polemical formulations over against the mythologies and religious beliefs of its environment.

15. 2Co 5:17; Gal 3:27-28. See my discussion of Galatians 3:27-28 in *Abusing Scripture: The Consequences of Misreading the Bible* (Downers Grove, IL: InterVarsity Press, 2009) pp.182-185. For a detailed and superb interpretation of the Pauline texts that, on the surface, seem to call for a hierarchical structure in the male-female relationship in home, church and society, I highly recommend Philip. B. Payne's *Man and Woman, One in Christ. An Exegetical and Theological Study of Paul's Letters* (Grand Rapids, MI: Zondervan, 2009).

Chapter 2: Intimate Friendship: How do we get there?

1. Jame Olthius "With-ing: A Psychotherapy of Love," *Journal of Psychology and Theology* 34 (2006): 66-77.

2. Anthony Hoekema, *Created in God's Image* (Grand Rapids: William B. Eerdmans Publishing Company, 1986).

3. James R. Beck and Bruce Demarest, *The Human Person in Theology*

and Psychology: A Biblical Anthropology for the Twenty-First Century (Grand Rapids: Kregel Publications, 2005).

4. See Janelle Kwee and Längle, Alfried, "Phenomenology in Psychotherapeutic Praxis: An Introduction to Personal Existential Analysis," *Experiencing EPIS, a Journal of the Existential and Psychoanalytic Institute and Society*, 2 (2013): 139-163; Alfried Längle, "The Viennese School of Existential Analysis. The search for Meaning and Affirmation of Life," in *Existential Therapy: Legacy, Vibrancy, and Dialogue*, ed. Barnett and Madison, (New York: Routledge, 2012), 159-170; and Viktor Frankl, *On the Theory and Therapy of Mental Disorders: An Introduction to Logotherapy and Existential Analysis* (New York: Brunner-Routledge, 2004).

5. Brené Brown, *Daring Greatly: How the Courage to be Vulnerable Transforms the Way we Live, Love, Parent, and Lead* (New York: Avery, 2012).

6. Carol Gilligan, *In A Different Voice* (Cambridge: Harvard University Press, 1982), and *The Birth of Pleasure (*New York: Knopf, 2002).

7. Sue Johnson, *Love Sense: The Revolutionary New Science of Romantic Relationships* (New York: Little Brown and Company, 2013), 4.

8. Henri Nouwen, *Reaching Out: The Three Movements of the Spiritual Life* (New York: Doubleday, 1975), 81.

9. John M. Gottman and Nan Silver, *The Seven Principles for Making Marriage Work* (New York: Harmony Books, 2015).

Chapter 3: Communicating as a Couple

1. John M. Gottman, and Nan Silver, *The Seven Principles for Making Marriage Work* (New York: Harmony, 2015), 3.

2. Robert L. Lees, *Prepared Companions: A Guide to Loving Relationships* (Ravensdale, WA: Idyll Arbor, 2004), 45.

3. Marshall B. Rosenberg, *Nonviolent Communication: A Language of Life*, 3rd. ed. (Encinitas, CA: Puddle Dancer Press, 2015), 127.

4. John M. Gottman, Julie Schwartz Gottman, and Joan DeClaire, "We Only Have Time for the Kids Now," in *10 Lessons to Transform Your Marriage: America's Love Lab Experts Share Their Strategies for Strengthening Your Relationship* (New York: Three Rivers Press, 2006), 241-242.

5. Gottman and Silver, *The Seven Principles for Making Marriage Work*.

6. Based on this information, Dr. Gottman can listen for just a few minutes to a couple in conflict and predict with an average of 91% accuracy whether a relationship is thriving or, without intervention, will end in divorce (Gottman and Silver, *Seven Principles,* 2).

7. The Four Horsemen concept and image was created by Drs. John and Julie Gottman. Re-printed with permission from The Gottman Institute. For additional resources, workshops and therapy for couples, visit www.gottman.com.

8. This information is primarily drawn from Gottman and Silver, *The Seven Principles for Making Marriage Work*.

9. Gottman and Silver, *Seven Principles,* 41.

10. Aída Besançon Spencer, William David Spencer, Steven R. Tracy, and Celestia G. Tracy, "Marriage Roles and Decision Making: Aída and Bill Spencer's Viewpoint," in *Marriage at the Crossroads: Couples in Conversation about Discipleship, Gender Roles, Decision Making and Intimacy* (Downers Grove, IL: IVP Academic, 2009).

11. Ibid., 101.

12. Ibid., 109.

13. Ibid., 109-110.

14. "The Art of Compromise" exercise was created by Drs. John and Julie Gottman, world-renowned researchers and psychologists in couples and family relationships. Re-printed with permission from The Gottman Institute. For additional resources, workshops, and therapy for couples, visit www.gottman.com.

15. "The Aftermath of a Fight" exercise was created by Drs. John and Julie Gottman, world-renowned researchers and psychologists in couples and family relationships. Re-printed with permission from The Gottman Institute. Copies available in booklet format. For additional resources, workshops, and therapy for couples, visit www.gottman.com.

Chapter 4: Money Matters

1. For help on being able to reach a decision, try the exercise "The Art of Compromise" in the chapter on Communicating as a Couple.

2. You can answer this question in part by reading the annual reports of the organization, looking for external validation like approval by the ECFA (Evangelical Council for Financial Accountability), and by requesting Form 990 of 990-PF that the organization is required to file with the IRS detailing the finances of the organization. The National Center for Charitable Statistics has online links to many Form 990's of 990-PF's (See: nccsweb.urban.org).

3. For groceries and household sundries that are purchased on a regular basis use a list to avoid the temptation to buy things you see that you don't need. Follow ads and buy in quantity for later use items on a

good sale or consider membership in a warehouse club where prices are generally lower. Use coupons if the coupons are for items you regularly use. Compare the price per ounce for different sizes and brands. Buy house brands rather than national brands if of comparable quality. Don't shop when you are hungry or tired. Try buying food in a less processed state (i.e. potatoes versus tater tots or potato chips) which is usually less expensive and is healthier for you. Try eating out less. Look for creative resourceful things that you can do like having your own garden or doing your own repairs or sewing to reduce the need to spend.

Chapter 5: Forgiveness, Apology, and Reconciliation

1. Smedes, Lewis B. Smedes, *The Art of Forgiving: When You Need to Forgive and Don't Know How* (New York: Ballantine Books, 1996), 171.

2. Lewis B. Smedes. BrainyQuote.com, Xplore Inc, 2016.

3. If a person is in trauma from an offense or multiple offenses, it is understandably hard to forgive. Oppression, abuse, or pain inflicted by another person create a level of psychological trauma. The effects of trauma are multifaceted and may include: periodic flashbacks, intrusive memories and dreams, efforts to avoid the memory, inability to sleep or concentrate, general limitations in functioning such as irritability, and inability to experience positive emotions.

4. Robert D. Enright, *Forgiveness is a Choice: A Step-by-Step Process for Resolving Anger and Restoring Hope* (Washington, DC: American Psychological Association, 2001), 273-4.

5. Lewis B. Smedes. BrainyQuote.com, Xplore Inc, 2016.

6. Sue Johnson, *Hold Me Tight: Seven Conversations for a Lifetime of Love* (New York: Little, Brown and Company, 2008).

7. I include statistics from multiple sources depicting the occurrences of domestic violence: 25% of women are victims of physical violence. See: Al Miles, *Domestic Violence: What Every Pastor Needs to Know* (Minneapolis: MN, 2000), 50; Jimmy Carter, *A Call to Action: Women, Religion, Violence, and Power* (New York: Simon & Schuster, 2014), 143; Ron Clark, *Setting the Captives Free: A Christian Theology for Domestic Violence* (Eugene, OR: Wipf & Stock, 2005), 234. 29% of women and 10% of men are victims (National Domestic Violence Hotline), 50% of women are victims when psychological abuse is included (Clark, 2005, Intro.xx), 50% of women and men are victims of psychological aggression (National Domestic Violence Hotline), and one in three women (The American Medical Association) reported by Lundy Bancroft, *Why Does He*

Do That: Inside the Minds of Angry and Controlling Men (New York: The Berkeley Publishing Group, 2002), 9. Three in ten Canadian women from Nancy Nason-Clark, *The Battered Wife: How Christians Confront Family Violence* (Louisville, Kentucky: Westminster John Knox Press, 1997) 6.

8. "...researchers in the field of family violence have consistently argued that abuse crosses all religious boundaries and that the rates inside and outside the walls of the church are similar." Catherine Clark Kroeger and Nancy Nason-Clark, *No Place for Abuse: Biblical & Practical Resources to Counteract Domestic Violence.* (Downer's Grove, IL: InterVarsity Press, 2010), 50.

9. Shirley P. Glass with Jean Coppock Staeheli, *Not "Just Friends:" Rebuilding Trust and Recovering Your Sanity After Infidelity* (New York: Free Press, 2003), 2.

10. Ibid., 340.

11. Ron Clark, *Setting the Captives Free: A Christian Theology for Domestic Violence* (Eugene, OR: Wipf & Stock, 2005), 173.

12. Al Miles, *Domestic Violence: What Every Pastor Needs to Know.* (Minneapolis, MN: Augsburg Fortress, 2000),130.

13. Al Miles*, Domestic Violence*

14. To illustrate the extended process of forgiveness, note that Everett Worthington, *Five Steps to Forgiveness: The Art and Science of Forgiving* (New York: Crown Publishers, 2001) presents a Five Step Model of Forgiveness. Robert D. Enright, *Forgiveness is a Choice: A Step-by-Step Process for Resolving Anger and Restoring Hope* (Washington, DC: American Psychological Association, 2001) has developed a Four Phase Guideline to Forgiving. The second half of Judith Herman, *Trauma and Recovery: The Aftermath of Violence- from Domestic Abuse to Political Terror* (New York: Basic Books, 1992) is devoted to stages of recovery after trauma.

15. Lewis B. Smedes, *Forgive and Forget: Healing the Hurts We Don't Deserve* (New York: HarperCollins Publishers, 1984), 45.

16. Everett Worthington, *Forgiving and Reconciling: Bridges to Wholeness and Hope* (Downer's Grove, IL: InterVarsity Press, 2003).

17. Everett Worthington, *Five Steps to Forgiveness: The Art and Science of Forgiving* (New York: Crown Publishers, 2001), 43.

18. Corrie ten Boom, "Corrie ten Boom on Forgiveness," *Guideposts,* November 1972, https://www.guideposts.org/better-living/positive-living/guideposts-classics-corrie-ten-boom-on-forgiveness.

19. Ibid.

20. *Merriam Webster Dictionary*, 1996, "repent."

21. Sue Johnson, *Hold Me Tight*, 176-177.

22. Lewis B. Smedes, *The Art of Forgiving* (New York: Ballantine Books, 1996).

Chapter 6: Sacred Sexuality

1. Ronald Rolheiser, *The Holy Longing: Search for a Christian Spirituality* (New York: Doubleday, 1999), 196.

2. James Wittstock, "Further Validation of the Sexual-Spiritual Integration Scale: Factor Structure and Relations to Spirituality and Psychological Integration" (unpublished dissertation, Loyola College, 2009).

3. The individuals in our research speak to the possibility and hope that we can live in freedom from shame. They shared about the darkness of sexual shame and their yearnings for change. They spoke about how their journey to healing was arduous, but worthwhile, leading to mutuality in their sexual relationships with their spouses. These journeys brought light into the dark spaces inside themselves; it revealed their longings for connection, intimacy, and freedom. For these men and women, resilience to sexual shame was, and is, developing over time and in relationship with others. It was in connection with themselves, their partners, their communities, and with their God that they have come to experience their sexuality differently. Longed-for life-giving messages about sexuality were birthed in them and their relationships. Now there are moments in which they are totally naked and vulnerable, and no longer feel the need to hide.

4. Deborah L. Tolman, Christin P. Bowman, and Breanne Fahs. "Sexuality and embodiment," in *APA Handbook of Sexuality and Psychology*, eds. Deborah Tolman, Lisa Diamond, Jose Bauermeister, William George, James Pfau and Monique Ward (Washington, DC: American Psychological Association, 2014), 759-804.

5. Judith Lewis Herman, "Shattered Shame States and Their Repair," in *Shattered States: Disorganised Attachment and its Repair*, eds. Kate White and Judy Yellin (London: Karnac Books, 2011), 157-170.

6. John Bradshaw, *Healing the Shame that Binds You: Recovery Classics Edition* (Deerfield Beach: Health Communications, 2005), 80.

7. Brené Brown, "Shame Resilience Theory: A Grounded Theory on Women and Shame," *Families in Society* 87, no. 1 (2006): 43-52, 45.

8. Brown, "Shame Resilience."

9. Rachel Held Evans, *The Year of Biblical Womanhood* (Nashville:Thomas Nelson, 2012), 7.

10. Judith Daniluk, "The Meaning and Experience of Female Sexuality," *Psychology of Women Quarterly* 17, (1993): 53-69.

11. James Wittstock, Ralph Piedmont, and Ciarrocchi, Joseph, "Developing a Scale to Measure the Integration of Sexuality and Spirituality" (unpublished manuscript, 2007).

12. Brown "Shame Resilience."

13. Ibid.

14. Tina Schermer Sellers, "Beloved Sex: Healing Shame and Restoring the Sacred in Sexuality," in *Sex, Gender, and Christianity,* eds. Priscilla Pope-Levison and John R. Levison (Eugene: Wipf and Stock Publishers, 2012), 218-235.

15. Herman, "Shattered Shame States."

16. Brené Brown, *The Gifts of Imperfection: Let Go of Who You Think You're Supposed to Be and Embrace Who You Are* (Centre City: Hazelden Publishing, 2010).

17. Ibid., 19

18. Kelly Murray, Joseph Ciarrocchi, and Nichole Murray-Swank, "Spirituality, Religiosity, Shame and Guilt as Predictors of Sexual Attitudes and Experiences," *Journal of Psychology and Theology* 35 (2007): 222-234.

19. Judith C. Daniluk and Nicolle Browne, "Traditional Religious Doctrine and Women's Sexuality: Reconciling the Contradictions," *Women & Therapy* 31, no. 1 (2008): 129-142.

20. Krystal M. Hernandez, Annette Mahoney, and Kenneth I. Pargament, "Sanctification of Sexuality: Implications for Newlyweds' Marital and Sexual Quality," *Journal of Family Psychology* 25, no. 5 (2011): 775-780.

21. Chuck M. MacKnee, "Profound Sexual and Spiritual Encounters Among Practicing Christians: A Phenomenological Analysis," *Journal of Psychology and Theology* 30, no. 3 (2002): 234-244.

22. Ibid., 234-244, 241.

Chapter 7: What about Headship?

1. E.g. Jerome regarding Eph 5:21, "Let the bishops hear these words, let the presbyters hear them, let every order of teachers hear them, that they be subjected to those who are subjected to themselves." PL 26: 654; R. Heine, ed. *The Commentaries of Origen and Jerome on St Paul's Epistle to the Ephesians* (Oxford: Oxford University Press, 2002) 232. 1 Clement 37:5–38:1, ca. AD 96, states that all members "are united in a

common subjection . . . let each be subject to his neighbor." Polycarp (ca. AD 70–155), To the Philippians 10.2 and Theodoret, Commentarius in omnes B. Pauli Epistolas, 2:33, affirm that "we must be subject to one another." Pope John Paul II writes in Mulieris Dignitatem ("On the Dignity of Women") n. 24, "in the relationship between husband and wife the 'subjection' is not one-sided but mutual."

2. Jerome cites without criticism the patristic understanding that according to Eph 5:21, "husbands are to be subject to their wives according to the duty which is commanded." PL 26: 654; Heine, Origen and Jerome, 232. Origen, (Heine 231–232): "Eph. 5:21 Being subject, he says, to one another in the fear of Christ. This completely destroys all desire to rule and be first." Chrysostom, Homily XIX on Ephesians, Nicene and Post-Nicene Fathers, Series 1, henceforth NPNF1, 13:142, "it were better that both masters and slaves be servants to one another . . . submit yourself; do not simply yield, but submit yourself. Entertain this feeling towards all, as if all were your masters." Cf. Homily X, "'submitting yourselves one to another in the fear of Christ'; – if I charge moreover the wife to fear and reverence her husband, although she is his equal; much more must I so speak to the servant."

3. Including NA28, NA27, UBS5, UBS4, Nestle, Westcott and Hort, Tasker, Souter, Alford, Tischendorf, and Goodrich and Lukaszewski (2003), following 𝔓46, Codex Vaticanus B, Clement of Alexandria (Stromata 4.8.64), Origen, Theodore of Mopsuestia, and Jerome's commentary and assertion that in Greek manuscripts verse 22 never repeats the verb "submit" from verse 21. J. Armitage Robinson cites Jerome's statement: "subditae sint of the Latin 'in Graecis codicibus non habitur'" in St. Paul's Epistle to the Ephesians (London: James Clarke, n.d.) 301. After "submit" first appears in Codex Sinaiticus ca. AD 350–360, every surviving New Testament manuscript includes "submit" in 5:22. Since none of the thousands of New Testament manuscripts after AD 350 removed it, removal can't reasonably explain why all the earliest manuscripts and citations of this verse omit "submit." Consequently, "submit" must not have been in Paul's original letter. Furthermore, "submit" occurs in some manuscripts after "wives" but in others after "husbands" and in either second ("you") or third person ("they"). Differences like these in word location and grammatical form are typical of later additions. Some translations even put the subject and object in verse 22 into a separate paragraph from their sentence's verb, which is in verse 21. This defies reason and is contrary to the text in all major editions

of the Greek New Testament. Even some prominent advocates of exclusive male leadership, agree that this sentence links the submission of wives to husbands to the principle of mutual submission (George W. Knight III, "Husbands and Wives as Analogues of Christ and the Church Ephesians 5:21-33 and Colossians 3:18-19" in *Recovering Biblical Manhood and Womanhood: A Response to Evangelical Feminism*, ed. by John Piper and Wayne Grudem (Wheaton, Ill.: Crossway, 1991), 165–167 and 492 n. 1; James B. Hurley, *Man and Woman in Biblical Perspective* (Grand Rapids: Zondervan, 1981) 139–141.) It is because verses 21–22 are part of the same sentence that Paul did not need to repeat "submit" in verse 22. "Submit" is assumed from verse 21.

4. This symmetry directly parallels Jesus' statements regarding divorce by a man or a woman recorded in Mk 10:9–12 and uses the same verb (*chōrizō*). This and "not the Lord" in v. 12, confirms that Paul is citing Jesus just as he does in his other explicit citations from Jesus, e.g., 1Co 9:14; 11:23–25; 1Th 4:15–17.

5. Richard B. Hays, *First Corinthians* (IBC; Louisville, KY: John Knox, 1997), 120 states, "there is no difference in the legal or practical effect of the action: the modern distinction between 'separation' and 'divorce' is not in view here, and Paul's formulation in verse 13 recognizes the woman's legal right to divorce her husband—though he is urging Christian women not to exercise it."

6. Cf. Marion L. Soards, *1 Corinthians* (NIBCNT; Peabody, MA: Hendrickson, 1999), 139.

7. Hays, *First Corinthians*, 131.

8. BDAG 783 1.d.β col 2.

9. BDAG 905.

10. Marcus Barth, *Ephesians* (Garden City, NY: Doubleday, 1974) 2: 618.

11. Henry George Liddell, Robert Scott, Henry Stuart Jones, Roderick McKenzie, *A Greek-English Lexicon With a Supplement* (Oxford: Clarendon Press, 1968) 945.

12. Nor do its supplements by E. A. Barber, *Supplement* (1968) 83, R. Renehan, *Greek Lexicographical Notes: A Critical Supplement to the Greek-English Lexicon of Liddell-Scott-Jones* (Hypomnemata 45; Göttingen: Vandenhoeck & Ruprecht, 1975) 120, or P. G. W. Glare with assistance by A. A. Thompson, *Revised Supplement* (1996) 175–176.

13. Including the dictionaries by Moulton and Milligan, Friedrich Preisigke, Pierre Chantraine, S. C. Woodhouse, and thirteen additional

dictionaries Richard S. Cervin cites in "Does Κεφαλή mean 'Source' or 'Authority Over' in Greek Literature? A Rebuttal," *Trinity Journal* 10 NS (1989): 85–112, 86–87.

14. Heinrich Schlier's article on *kephalē* in the *Theological Dictionary of the New Testament* (Grand Rapids: Eerdmans, 1965) 3:674.

15. The number 171 does not include instances where *kephalē* means "first" in sequence (1Ch 12:9; 23:8, 11, 19, 20; 24:21; 26:10 twice, all translated "first" in the NASB) or "top" spatially (e.g., Jdg 16:3 NASB).

16. The reason this number is not higher is that some Hebrew expressions using "head" meaning "leader" are not natural expressions in English, like "head priest," which the NASB translates "chief priest."

17. The one clear instance is Isa 7:9b, "the head of Samaria is the son of Remalia." In each of the other alleged instances, the standard LXX text either did not translate "head" *kephalē*, or *kephalē* is not used clearly as a metaphor meaning "leader." Alfred Rahlfs, *Septuaginta* (Stuttgart: Würtembergische Bibelanstalt) 2:574 identifies "The head of Damascus is Rasim" as not in the LXX but added to Isa 7:8a by Origen in the third century AD, long after Paul. Consequently, it could not influence how Paul or his readers understood "head." Isa 7:8–9 uses *kephalē* twice to mean "capital city," but cities are not leaders, nor do they have authority. The LXX explains four reference to "head-tail" idioms to mean things other than "leader": "above and below" (Dt 28:13), "high and low" (Dt 28:43–44), "great and small" (Isa 9:143) or "beginning and end" (Isa 19:15). In Isa 9:143 LXX "great and small," replaces the Hebrew, "palm branch and reed." "Head" must not mean "leader" in Isa 9:143 since v. 154 explains the "head" to be "the old man and flatterers" and "the tail" to be "the lying prophets." Isa 9:154 does not translate the Hebrew "head" with *kephalē* but with *archē*, here meaning "beginning." The old men and flatters are the beginning of those the Lord takes away from Israel along with the lying prophets. In order to preserve the original Hebrew contrast between "head" and "tail," these four could hardly be translated without *kephalē*. Wayne Grudem, "The Meaning of *Kephalē* ('Head'): A Response to Recent Studies," Appendix 1 of *Biblical Manhood and Womanhood*, 425–468, 441–442, alleges one other occurrence, 3 Kingdoms (1Ki) 8:1, apparently unaware that Rahlfs LXX 1:646 identifies it, too, as added by Origen (d. ca. 254). In any event, "heads" in 1Ki 8:1 means "tops," not "leaders": "Solomon assembled all the elders of Israel with all the tops (kephalas) of the staffs of the fathers of the sons of Israel lifted up before king Solomon." The term for staffs

refers to actual staffs even where the staff is a staff of office or scepter (LSJ 1562). Grudem appeals to BDB 641, but the LXX translates all references to "tribe" with a different word, phulē. Grudem's translation "tribes" makes no sense here: "with all the heads of the tribes of the fathers of the sons of Israel lifted up."

18. Peter Walters, *The Text of the Septuagint: Its Corruptions and Their Emendations,* ed. D. W. Gooding (Cambridge: Cambridge Univ. Press, 1973), 143.

19. In four more passages the standard LXX translation has *eis kephalēn.* The only English equivalent for *eis kephalēn* that fits these contexts naturally is "as head." None of the other English equivalents for *eis* BDAG 288–291 lists sounds natural in these passages: "into, in, toward, to, at, until, on, for, throughout, up to, in order to, with respect to, with reference to, by, with, or in the face of." The four are: Jdg 11:11; 2 Kingdoms (= 2Sa) 22:44; Ps 17:44 = 18:44 in Hebrew = 18:43 in English; La 1:5. In addition to these, three variant reading of "as head" (*eis kephalēn*) meaning "as leader" occur in only one manuscript, Codex Alexandrinus. All three occur in a single ten verse span, Jdg 10:18; 11:8, 9. A single scribe almost certainly translated all three of these variants. This scribe chose the most literal translation, perhaps influenced by "as head" in Jdg 11:11. These three should not be regarded as part of the LXX text since they are not in the older, more standard, LXX texts. Each of these three verses in Codex Vaticanus and Codex Sinaiticus (in 10:18; its surviving text goes only to 11:2) has "ruler" (*archonta*) instead of "head" (*kephalē*). Since "head" is the more obvious equivalent for the Hebrew word "head," "ruler" in Vaticanus and Sinaiticus shows that their texts' translator(s) regarded "ruler" to be a more appropriate translation than "head" when "head" in Hebrew conveyed "leader."

"As" (*eis*) in each of these cases translates a letter of the Hebrew alphabet called "lamed" prefixed to "head." In all four cases, John R. Kohlenberger III, ed. *NIV Interlinear Hebrew-English Old Testament* (4 vols.; Grand Rapids: Zondervan, 1982) translates the lamed "as," cf. BDB 512 II.2 e. H. E. Dana and Julius R. Mantey, *A Manual Grammar of the Greek New Testament* (Toronto: Macmillan, 1957) 103 identifies *eis* meaning "as, expressing equivalence," citing passages like Heb 1:5 "as a son" and "as a father," Mk 10: 8 "as one flesh," and Ac 7:53 "as delivered by angels"). Nigel Turner cites *eis* meaning "as like normal Greek *hōs*," e.g. Mt 21:46 "as a prophet" in *A Grammar of New Testament Greek. Vol. III Syntax,* ed. James Hope Moulton (Edinburgh: T&T Clark, 1963) 247. BDAG

290 4.d cites "as a witness" in Jas 5:3, "as servants" in Heb 1:14, and "tongues are as a sign" in 1Co14:22. BAG 229–230 4.d. and 8.b. cite "as her own son" in Ac 7:21 and "as a light for the Gentiles" in Ac 13:47. In light of the inclusion of "as" (*eis*) and all the evidence that "leader" was not a standard meaning of *kephalē*, most Greek readers of the LXX probably understood each of these four references to *eis kephalēn* as a simile "as head," not a metaphor, "is head." They would either understand them as comparisons to a literal head or would interpret "head" with a standard Greek meaning for "head" that fits the context, such as "top," "noblest part," or "source" (cf. LSJ 945; Philip B. Payne, *Man and Woman, One in Christ: An Exegetical and Theological Study of Paul's Letters* (Grand Rapids: Zondervan, 2009)123–137, 283–290) of something. The presence of *eis* makes these four passages read far more smoothly for Greek readers who did not naturally associate "head" with "leader." The English translation of the KJV, ASV and *The Septuagint Version of the Old Testament with an English Translation* (Grand Rapids: Zondervan, 1970), 333, 436, 708, 972 simply omit the preposition in all four of these *eis kephalēn* passages, as do the RSV, NIV, NRSV, and ESV in all but one case, because in English, unlike Greek, "head" by itself usually conveys leader.

20. Paul uses apposition twice here, first to define "the body" as "the church," and second, to define "the head" as "the source" by identifying "he is the head" with "who is the source."

21. A. T. Robertson, *A Grammar of the Greek New Testament in the Light of Historical Research* (Nashville: Broadman, 1934), 399 identifies this as "emphatic apposition since the grammatical construction of each of the four parts of the parallel expressions matches exactly:

1. nominative singular subject (Christ = he)
2. predicate nominative singular noun describing the subject ("savior" explains "head")
3. genitive singular article ("of the" = "of the")
4. genitive singular noun identifying what Christ saves ("the church" = "the body")."

22. E.g. the ASV, NASB, CEB, AMP, AMPC, DLNT, NABRE, NET Bible, OJB, TLV, and WEB.

23. Paul never even uses the word "savior" in his earlier letters, Gal, 1–2 Th, 1–2Co, and Ro, so it is speculative to interpret "savior" as a title in Eph 5. The NIV inserts "the" before "husband," "head," and "Savior," though none of these have an article in the Greek.

24. Barth, *Ephesians*, 1:184; Gregory W. Dawes, *The Body in Question: Meaning and Metaphor in the Interpretation of Ephesians 5:21–33* (Leiden: Brill, 1998), 147, argues that "head" in 4:15 is a metaphor for "source of the body's life and growth."

25. Cf. BDAG 296–297, ἐκ 3, "denoting origin, cause, motive, reason . . . source fr. which someth. flows or comes."

26. 1 Corinthians 11:3 (3x), 4, 5; Ephesians 4:15; 5:23; Colossians 1:18; 2:19. See Payne, Man and Woman, 115–139, 271–290.

27. The context of Eph 1:22 ("far above . . . over") supports the meaning "top." "Top" or "crown" also fits the parallel wording in Col 2:10.

28. "And who will endure this?" *Hom. in ep. 1 ad Cor.* 26.3 in NPNF1, 12:150.

Chapter 8: What about Abuse?

1. "Facts About Domestic Violence and Sexual Abuse," National Coalition Against Domestic Violence, 2015, https://www.ncadv.org/files/Domestic%20Violence%20and%20Sexual%20Abuse%20NCADV.pdf.

2. "Domestic Violence," The United States Department of Justice, last modified June 16, 2017, https://www.justice.gov/ovw/domestic-violence.

3. "Report of the Attorney General's National Task Force on Children Exposed to Violence," U.S. Department of Justice, December 12, 2012, https://www.justice.gov/defendingchildhood/cev-rpt-full.pdf.

4. "Statistics," National Coalition Against Domestic Violence, http://www.ncadv.org/learn-more/statistics

5. Ericka Kimball, "Edleson Revisited: Reviewing Children's Witnessing of Domestic Violence 15 Years Later," *Journal of Family Violence (*November 2015), https://www.researchgate.net/publication/284803972_Edleson_Revisited_Reviewing_Children%27s_Witnessing_of_Domestic_Violence_15_Years_Later.

Chapter 9: What about Divorce?

1. These debates are recorded at Mishnah Gittin 9.10; Sifré Deut.269; Jerusalem Talmud Sotah 1.1, 1a.

2. As seen by the misunderstanding of Shammaite teaching by R. Yose b. Zabida in Jerusalem Talmud Sotah 1.1, 1a.

3. Mishnah Gittin 9.10.

4. Mishnah Ketuvot 5.5,8.

5. Mishnah Ketuvot 5.6

6. David Instone-Brewer, "Jewish Women Divorcing Their Husbands

in Early Judaism: The Background to Papyrus Se'elim 13," *Harvard Theological Review* 92 (1999): 349-57.

7. Legally, neglect was considered a lesser offence because it was included in the law of abandonment. Not giving enough food or clothing was considered a lesser offense than giving none.

Appendix: Inter-Testamental Background Regarding Jewish and Early Christian Views about Women

1. Translations from R. H. Charles, ed., *The Apocrypha and Pseudepigrapha of the Old Testament: The Apocrypha*, Vol I (Oxford: The Clarendon Press, 1913; reprint 1969)

2. Charles, *Pseudepigrapha*, Vol. II. (3. 2 and 32.1).

3. Craig S. Keener, *Paul, Women and Wives: Marriage and Women's Ministry in the Letters of Paul* (Peabody, Mass: Hendrickson Publishers, 1992), documents this Rabbinic tradition throughout his study (e.g., pp. 83-84 and notes.

4. Philo, *Questions and Answers on Genesis*. Supplement I. Loeb Classical Library (Cambridge: Harvard University Press, 1937).

5. *Jewish Antiquities* 4.8.15, par. 219 in Loeb Classical Library

6. Paul reflects this formula in Gal 3:28. See Leon Morris, *Galatians. Paul's Charter of Christian Freedom* (Downers Grove, IL: InterVarsity Press, 1996), p. 121, and F. F. Bruce, *The Epistle to the Galatians: A Commentary on the Greek Text* (Grand Rapids, MI: Eerdmans, 1982), p. 187, who cites both the Rabbinic sources for this three-fold formula of superior social, racial and gender structure, as well as similar formulations in Greek literature.

7. See Frank and Evelyn Stagg, *Women in the World of Jesus* (Philadelphia, PA: Westminster Press, 1978), and Joachim Jeremias, *Jerusalem in the Time of Jesus: An Investigation into Economic and Social Conditions During the New Testament Period* (Philadelphia, PA: Augsburg Fortress, 1979).

8. Charles, *Pseudepigrapha*, Vol. II.

9. Andrew Louth, ed., Genesis1-11. *Ancient Christian Commentary on Scripture. Old Testament I* (Downers Grove, IL: InterVarsity Press, 2001), p. 78.

10. Ibid., p. 68.

11. Gerald Bray, ed., *1-2 Corinthians*. Ancient Christian Commentary on the Scripture. New Testament, Vol. VII (Downers

Grove, IL: InterVarsity Press, 1999), p. 105.
  12. Ibid., p. 107
  13. bid., p. 109

About the Contributors

Ch 1

Dr. Manfred T. Brauch is the author of numerous essays in both popular and academic Christian journals, as well as several books, including *Hard Sayings of Paul*, and *Abusing Scripture: The Consequences of Misreading the Bible*. After retirement from Eastern Baptist Theological, Manfred and his wife, Marjean, have engaged in volunteer work in medical mission and theological/biblical education.

ch 9

Rev. Dr. David Instone-Brewer is the Senior Research Fellow in Rabbinics and the New Testament at Tyndale House, Cambridge. His academic interests center on Jewish background and the Greek/Hebrew text of the Bible. He is kept sane by a wife, two daughters and by watching low-brow movies.

Ch 2 + 6-sexuality

Janelle Kwee is a Registered Psychologist (BC and WA, USA) and has been actively involved since 2006 in training and mentoring future psychologists and psychotherapists through university faculty appointments in graduate professional programs at Wheaton College and at Trinity Western University. She is married to Dr. Alex Kwee, and has two wonderful children. She enjoys traveling and spending time with family.

Ch 2

Hillary McBride, MA, RCC, is a therapist working in private practice in Vancouver, BC. She is a PhD candidate in Counseling Psychology at the University of British Columbia. She speaks and does workshops regularly on the intersection of mental health and spirituality, women's sexuality, sex therapy, and feminist psychology. In 2017 she released a book called *Mothers, Daughters, and Body Image: Learning to Love Ourselves as We Are.*

Ch 8 – Abuse

Dr. Nancy Murphy has served as Executive Director of Northwest Family Life Learning and Counseling Center (NWFL) since 1994. Based in Seattle, Washington, NWFL is a faith based, non-profit agency dedicated to assisting individuals and families in finding hope and healing when facing the pain of domestic violence, trauma and related issues. She is an Adjunct Professor at The Seattle School of Theology and Psychology.

Dr. David M. Nelson is Professor of Economics at Western Washington University. David helped begin the Western Washington University Christian Faculty Forum to support, encourage, and equip Christian faculty to better fulfill their roles as Christ followers and as university professors. He and his wife Lynne have been married over forty years and have four children, four grandchildren, and many sponsored-children in the third world.

Lynne Nelson has a BA in psychology from the University of Oregon and an MC from Trinity Western University. She is a licensed mental health counselor in private practice in Bellingham, Washington where she has a passion for helping others by walking with them on their journey as they seek growth and authenticity. Lynne and her husband, Dave, have been married over 40 years. They enjoy time with their four adult children and four grandchildren. Other interests include reading, traveling, hiking, and swimming.

Philip Barton Payne, PhD in New Testament from the University of Cambridge, is well known for his studies on New Testament textual criticism, the parables of Jesus, and man and woman in Paul's letters, especially his book, *Man and Woman, One in Christ*. Phil and his wife Nancy have three married children and five grandchildren. They all love the Lord.

Ch 6 sexuality

Kelsey Siemens attended Trinity Western University, where she obtained an MA in Counseling Psychology. She is currently practicing as a Registered Clinical Counselor at a private practice in Langley, BC, Canada, specializing in sexuality and trauma.

CPSIA information can be obtained
at www.ICGtesting.com
Printed in the USA
BVHW04s1529080418
512464BV00002BA/142/P